Aging Parents,
Aging Children

Aging Parents, Aging Children

How to Stay Sane and Survive

Miriam K. Aronson Ed.D and Marcella Bakur Weiner Ph.D.

ROWMAN & LITTLEFIELD PUBLISHERS, INC.
Lanham • Boulder • New York • Toronto • Plymouth, UK

ROWMAN & LITTLEFIELD PUBLISHERS, INC.

Published in the United States of America
by Rowman & Littlefield Publishers, Inc.
A wholly owned subsidary of The Rowman & Littlefield Publishing Group, Inc.
4501 Forbes Boulevard, Suite 200, Lanham, Maryland 20706
www.rowmanlittlefield.com

Estover Road
Plymouth PL6 7PY
United Kingdom

British Library Cataloguing in Publication Information Available

Library of Congress Cataloging-in-Publication Data

Aronson, Miriam K.
 Aging parents, aging children : how to stay sane and survive / Miriam K. Aronson and
Marcella Bakur Weiner.
     p. cm.
 Includes index.
 ISBN-13: 978-0-7425-4746-9 (pbk. : alk. paper)
 ISBN-10: 0-7425-4746-9 (pbk. : alk. paper)
 1. Parent and adult child—Handbooks, manuals, etc. 2. Caregivers—Handbooks,
manuals, etc. I. Weiner, Marcella Bakur II. Title.
 HQ755.86.A76 2007
 649.8084'6—dc22   2006020197

Printed in the United States of America

⊗™ The paper used in this publication meets the minimum requirements of American
National Standard for Information Sciences—Permanence of Paper for Printed Library
Materials, ANSI/NISO Z39.48-1992.

To my children and grandchildren who are a constant source of enrichment and joy.

—Miriam Aronson

To my husband, Wilhelm, who enlightens my aging by his radiance of being.

—Marcella Bakur Weiner

Contents

Foreword

Gary J. Kennedy, M.D.,
Director of Geriatric Psychiatry,
Montefiore Medical Center,
Albert Einstein College of Medicine

In *Aging Parents, Aging Children*, Drs. Aronson and Weiner focus on the family drama of old age. And they populate the play with the whole cast of characters from the admirable to the unlovable. Their theme is the intergenerational paradox of interdependence among ostensibly autonomous aged parents and their aging children. Indeed the changing quality of independence and what it takes to remain so into advanced age looms large in every American family. Today an octogenarian may have children in their sixties, grandchildren in their forties and great-grandchildren in their twenties. As a result the lessons learned from the seniormost family members will resonate for generations to come for good or ill. The impact on our personal expectations of age as well as our social and health policies will be enormous. And because the phenomenon of so many aged parents among us is so new it is important that we as actors receive a bit of direction rather than constantly having to improvise. It is in this way that *Aging Parents, Aging Children* will make its contribution.

The authors acknowledge that many if not most children manage to care for parents in need with remarkable ingenuity and skill. They are the natural caregivers that have inspired and educated the authors. Yet even the most natural of caregivers will face the inevitable mismatch between their skills and resources and their aged parents' needs and preferences at the end of the life span. The authors address this conflict with practical examples and vivid scenarios. In one particularly apt metaphor they compare a woman sandwiched between the unrelenting demands of a parent and the ever-present needs of herself and her children as a "peanut butter and jelly sandwich." Their advice is to stop being the jelly yielding to her parent's unreasonable pressure and start being the peanut butter, sticking to her needs.

However, this is not a work championing children's self-indulgence. Instead, most of the chapters seek to expand caregivers' repertoires and flexibility rather than exhort them to greater endurance. They discuss the children's unavoidable guilty feelings following a parent's entry into a nursing home as well as the rage when inflexible parents are unable to preserve the larger portion of their independence by delegating smaller parts of their autonomy. The satisfactions and the challenges of caregiving are discussed with humor and feeling.

The first chapter focuses on the diversity of families, caregivers and seniors with an emphasis on the inevitable decline in health and vitality associated with advanced age. The predominance of women among caregivers and the variety of meanings attached to being an adult-child caregiver are reviewed with an appreciation for both universal and unique features. The second chapter explores the personal beliefs, philosophies and personality traits that shape the caregiver process. The blending, even confounding of family relationships through second and third marriages is discussed as a new developmental task families will need to master as active life spans continue to grow. The authors also review how fitting of personality traits to the caregiver circumstances can reduce conflict as well as strengthen family ties. Discussion on the misfortune of pain in late life and the management of end-of-life care will be particularly informative for caregivers unaware of the substantial hospice and palliative care services available to assist both patient and family. In chapter 3, family dynamics and the variety of family configurations are discussed with attention paid to new traditions and new realities. Harmony and discord, rivalry and teamwork, and maturation of the caregiving experience are also discussed.

Chapter 4 urges the child caregiver to step back and assess the parent's situation from the perspectives of acute to chronic illness, both mental and physical. The assessment process identifies needs as well as avenues of help, which here and elsewhere in the book are described in jargon-free language. The need for a long-term perspective is emphasized with a reminder that widowhood will be a reality for the majority of older women. Chapter 5 builds on the assessment process to highlight the hard work of creating a care-plan blueprint starting with an open dialogue among family members. The outcome of a family conference will be recognition of differences and delegation of authority and responsibility. Here, Aronson and Weiner seek to prepare for undesirable contingencies that are predictable and need not take on crisis proportions if plans are in place beforehand. Attention to the pragmatic details of parent transportation, child proximity, and the need to revise the plans is emphasized.

Chapter 6 describes the financial impact of declining parental independence and various mechanisms to avert the tragedy of resources made unavailable to support the senior's needs. Specific legal procedures to ensure that the parent's assets are preserved for the parent's well-being would be a separate monograph. Instead, the authors alert child caregivers to the critical role that asset management has to play in providing for care over a period of dependency that the senior may never have anticipated. Chapter 7 is a brief overview of caregiver depression, and the range of care settings and arrangements that have arisen in response to the epidemic of Alzheimer's disease. Here again, the approach is revelatory rather than exhaustive, meant to steer the caregiver in the right direction rather than a final destination. Chapter 8 takes the reader on the "road to placement," meaning the senior's transition to facility-based living. From the initial decision to surrender the parent's residence all the way to tips on making successful visits to the nursing home, readers will find valuable insights and suggestions. They will also be reminded that placement solves some problems but will create others as well.

Chapter 9 diplomatically discusses those rare parents who are on the difficult side, some of whom are simply impossible. The authors' respect for the older individual's dignity is uppermost. They offer the reminder that the caregiving child's best efforts may not achieve the desired results but are for many a rewarding act of devotion. Chapter 10 covers the array of emotional responses to caregiving. Emotional reactions may be automatic, even involuntary, but their consequences need not be. A better understanding of the commonality of difficult feelings associated with the caregiving role can lead to less persistent distress. The authors' insight into the premature bereavement experienced by child caregivers for parents with dementia is but one example. Chapter 11 is written to provide the caregiver with insights into the self as well as techniques to restore personal equilibrium. The result is not less caregiving but rather better caregiving. And to close, chapter 12 is a condensed version of elements drawn from other sections.

In summary, *Aging Parents, Aging Children* is not the single source of everything a child caregiver needs to know. Neither is it a self-help manual for those overwhelmed with parent care. Rather, it is written for the average person faced with the caregiving challenge. Most will do fine with the resources at hand. More will do better having read the experiences of Drs. Aronson and Weiner.

Preface

*T*oday, there are more elders alive at one time than at any other time in human history. And every day, five thousand more individuals are turning sixty five. An aging boom is occurring thanks to advances in health care and technology and presents economic, social, political and personal challenges for our society.

A normal process, aging is unpredictable and varies from person to person. Aging changes are confounded and compounded by disease. Older individuals range from titans of society to totally dependent individuals, and their needs differ. For those needing help with their daily activities, family members are the primary source of aid.

Family caregivers are, in fact, the foundation of the chronic-care system with an estimated forty-four million Americans caring for an older or disabled relative. This informal care would cost almost $250 billion a year, if provided by paid caregivers, and its economic value is estimated to be more than 20 percent of our national health-care expenditures. This staggering amount of eldercare will increase dramatically with the projected continuation of the "graying" of the population.

Who are the heroes and heroines who do this caring? It is you, the adult child with children of your own and with career and financial pressures more intense than your parents could ever have dreamed about. You always knew they would get older, but that was later on, not to be thought about until another time. But that time has come sooner than you thought and, with it, a seemingly huge morass of dilemmas and choices, with few role models and confusing information.

This book is for you. In it we attempt to make you aware of some of the challenges you are likely to face as you and your eldercare recipient interact in the caregiving realm. And being sandwiched between the urgent needs of your elders and those of your children, it is easy to lose focus on your own sanity and survival. We remind you that there is a balance to be struck between providing effective care for another and staying true to your self. The key is to develop a plan that accommodates the philosophy, beliefs, preferences, personality traits, lifestyle and needs of both of you.

This book is liberally sprinkled with case vignettes from our clinical experience, with some details changed to protect confidentiality. While we may not provide you with an exact replica of your situation, our hope is that you will find examples that will be familiar and will reassure you that you are not alone and help is available. Ideally, while gaining increased self-awareness as well as practical information, you will realize that you do have choices.

The truth is that the caregiving experience, with its pressures and frustrations, is not all negative. A healthy approach will enable you to examine the situation and needs of your elderly relative while gaining awareness about yourself. We encourage you to view the caregiving process as a positive growth experience that may place you on an easier path toward your own later years.

Caregivers have, unexpectedly and under duress, developed or improved their skills in time management, financial planning, interpersonal relationships and, most critically, their own self-care. Navigating the maze of systems and services, resolving old conflicts and confronting their emotions has, they discovered, improved relationships with parents, siblings, spouses, partners, children and other relatives.

So, as you turn these pages, do so with an open mind. You may not see yourself in any single case but in a combination of several. Or conversely, you may find your situation described in detail. Whatever the case, it is our goal that you gain insight, confidence, compassion and hope that will guide you now and in your own later years.

Disclaimer: To protect the privacy of those who have shared their experiences with us, names and some other details have been altered.

Acknowledgments

Our deep appreciation goes to those older persons and their families whose experiences, concerns, struggles and triumphs we have shared and whose courage and resilience have taught us so much over the years.

To our families, friends and colleagues, we thank you for your encouragement to write this book and your valuable suggestions.

To Ross Miller, Art Pomponio and Jason Aronson at Rowman & Littlefield, we are grateful for your confidence in us.

To the expert editorial, production and marketing staff at Rowman & Littlefield, we are indebted to you for your enthusiasm and hard work.

To Joyce Varghese, we could not have finished this manuscript without your expert and cheerful computer assistance.

• 1 •

The Sandwiched

Old age is like a plane flying through a storm,
Once you're aboard, there is nothing you can
Do about it.

—Golda Meir

*L*ongevity is in. Face it, we're all getting older. Baby Boomers are today's hot topic, but in fact, this "boom" is occurring on the heels of an "aging explosion." Living past age 100 is no longer a teaser to be used for a television ad. Demographers now describe those 110 and over as "supercentenarians." Remarkably, these people's lives have spanned three centuries.

THE SANDWICH GENERATION

An undeniable trend over the past decades is that with college, graduate school and often marrying later, children are supported for much longer than were their parents' generation. With the aging explosion, the average woman has now been thrown into providing extended parent care, spending more time than she did in child care. Families are the backbone of care for the elderly and children, and appropriately, this generation of middle-aged adults has been labeled "the sandwich generation," caught between the needs of their children and their elderly parents. Sandy was one such person.

1

Sandy: In the Sandwich

In her early fifties, Sandy is an only child, a professional with an attentive husband, a married daughter expecting her first child and a son completing college. Sandy was always close to her now eighty-year-old mother, Marie. Widowed for ten years, Marie was proud of her independence and had insisted on continuing to live where she was, repeating, "This is my home and always will be." Sandy and her husband, Frank, were admiring of Marie's assertiveness and, even at times, stoicism. And then, this thread, seemingly strong and unending, broke. Unanswered phone calls panicked Sandy, who rushed to her mother's apartment, only to find her on the bathroom floor. Marie had fallen and broken her hip. Nobody was quite sure when. Sandy called 9-1-1. In that moment, her life changed.

Marie underwent hip surgery, after which she became confused. Within a few days, the hospital discharge planner, "just doing her job," was bombarding Sandy with questions such as "What are your plans for your mother?" "What kind of insurance does she have?" "Is she going some place for rehabilitation?" "If she does go home, who will be there to care for her?" Sandy panicked. Unable to focus, she went blank. As if from far away, she heard the final question, "And what about her dementia?" Sandy felt intense anger and responded, "Dementia? You may not know this, but my mother read the New York Times every day and did their crossword puzzles."

With her life spilling over, Sandy realized that she needed to find viable answers. With Marie's wishes uppermost in their minds, Sandy and Frank carefully reflected upon all that Marie had ever told them: "If anything ever happens to me, I want to be cared for in my own home. With help, if I need it. But, understand, I don't want to be a burden." While Sandy sobbed and Frank held her, they both accepted the reality of the situation and would honor Marie's preferences, no matter what.

It was obvious that it was Sandy who would have to allocate much of her time to being the primary caregiver. Frank would pitch in, the children would help, but basically, it all boiled down to her. Someone had to be in charge: the planner, the manager and the overall coordinator. Imagine a play where she and she alone is the lead player, using "understudies" only on emergency call. Sandy also realized that to keep her sanity, she would have to squeeze out time for herself—and for Frank, and for her children, and for her job. Pulling together the fragmented pieces of her self, she became determined to be the Humpty Dumpty who would not fall.

While Sandy was abruptly thrust into a caregiving role she never anticipated, there were many strong points in her life—a close relationship with her mother, a solid marriage, children who could and would assist and available financial resources. Nonetheless, Sandy's life was changed.

CHANGING FAMILY STRUCTURES

Family constellations are not what they used to be. While the traditional nuclear family, such as that of Sandy and Frank, is still very much among us, there are variations: the single person, the blended family, the single-parent family, the gay family and grandparents raising grandchildren. Eldercare responsibilities weigh differently on each of these configurations. For example, the never-married person living alone assumes caregiving responsibilities with little or no household support. The gay family may experience added strain due to prejudices and emotional upheavals that interfere with what needs to be done. Blended families, resulting from divorce or widowhood and remarriage, often have increased numbers of parents and grandparents—four or more sets of each, thus increasing both the caregiving responsibilities and the potential for familial conflict. Siblings and stepsiblings may have different values. The single parent may experience added pressures heaped upon an overflowing plate. For the caregiving relative with health issues themselves, such as arthritis, heart disease, diabetes, osteoporosis or asthma, the added strains may compromise their own health. Coping with these situations is like being part of an unwieldy, bulky hero sandwich. You now have not only the pressures from without but the pressures from within as well.

ALL FAMILIES ARE NOT ALIKE

While the "idyllic" family is a harmonious network of collaboration and cooperation, this is not always the case. All members do not necessarily have the same values and preferences. For instance, when it comes time to bring in professional home care or to move mom to a more supportive environment, disputes may flare. Said one daughter, cryptically, "Maybe it would be better if there were only one child. That way I could do what I know is right and get needed care for mom, since she's having such a hard time at home alone. Although mom prepared legal documents appointing me to be in charge, my siblings are having big problems with that, making me crazy and pushing my guilt button."

Parents have their own ways and sometimes stubborn beliefs, preferences and prejudices. Not all parents were model parents. Family history may repeat itself and old conflicts re-emerge. But sometimes, old conflicts can be remolded in a new way to create peace. Such was the case with Philip and Sam.

Sam: Putting Old Conflicts Aside

Sam and his partner, Philip, own an antique store. Three years ago, they adopted a child from Bulgaria. They named him Adam and began to provide a tender, loving family for him in their elegant townhouse in an upscale community. Taking turns caring for Adam, they set up a viable work routine, using occasional babysitters to fill the gaps. While Philip's parents are loving grandparents, Sam's are distant, never having come to terms with his homosexuality.

One day, Sam received a call from his sister, Molly, telling him that his father had suffered a massive stroke, rendering him paralyzed on the right side of his body and unable to speak. All professionals consulted agreed that there was little hope for complete recovery. Single and living on a limited income, Molly is a teacher who was never very close to her parents or her brother, though at times she was willing to babysit for Adam. Now, she is pleading with Sam to help her, as the situation is getting out of control.

Sam is of two minds. While he is angry at his parents for his rejection, he is, at the same time, now a parent himself. Although he would never reject his son, no matter what his lifestyle, how would Adam treat him in the same situation? Feeling that he must do something now, Sam decides to be supportive and at Molly's side. Her parents are his parents. And he has to be a role model for Adam. His own ambivalent feelings were put aside.

Sometimes, the care recipient is not a parent, but you jump in just the same, as with Rhonda and her uncle, Lenny.

Lenny: Difficult and Alone

In his professional life, Lenny was very successful and well known for his achievements, despite being obstreperous and self-absorbed. A widower, Lenny grew more and more difficult with age and even more so as he developed a dementia. Dementia is a brain condition that impairs memory, learning and judgment, severe enough to interfere with daily living. Personality and behavior are also affected, although not everyone becomes difficult.

As his dementia progressed, he became unable to manage on his own, and home care was begun. Because of his nastiness and resistance, the home-care workers, when they could be found, quickly burned out, eventually leading to a revolving door of caregivers. Desperate, his niece, Rhonda, the only one who seemed to have any attachment to him at all, spent time and energy researching a good facility, and Lenny was placed in what she thought to be the best. Predictably, he complained and complained and complained. Everyone and everything was no good—"No one cared, no one came, the food was disgusting, the doctors were stupid and nothing was right." Further, becoming paranoid, he insisted that "the CIA came in and stole everything."

For Rhonda, the caregiving had not ceased; rather, it just changed. The recipient of unending cranky phone calls and personal insults, she hung in. At the facility, the staff shrugged and said, "Oh, we know he's difficult. He can't help it." Staying through it all, Rhonda found excuses: "He doesn't know what he's doing. Look at how famous he was. I remember him as a little girl, when he gave me this sweet, sweet bracelet. I have it to this day."

That Rhonda stayed attached was her choice. Her memories of the past being the balm that heals, she became the primary, if only, visitor in his life, until the very end.

ALL ELDERS ARE NOT ALIKE

Some older persons are well, some are frail and some are very disabled. Their functioning ranges from independent to dependent. And their individual perceptions of what constitutes "old" are related to how they feel and how they function. Adding to this heterogeneity is the fact that there is more than one generation of elderly alive at the same time. A daughter of 65 may have a mother of 85 and a grandmother of 102, all residing under the same roof or in disparate places. Any or all may be caregivers or care recipients.

WELL ELDERS

The "well" elder may have one or several chronic ailments. Despite this, he or she remains active and high functioning, having gradually made necessary adaptations to any limitations. They may reside in their long-standing residence or may have moved to another area. Able to get around and do their daily activities, they may be continuing their life's work or retired—and trying to stay healthy and feel good.

Retirement may include embarking on a new career, attending school, pursuing hobbies or doing volunteer work. Jason, at sixty-four, retired from his insurance business and became an independent investment advisor, a second career he passionately loved. At seventy-four, Isabella, a retired seamstress, helped her daughter to develop a sought-after line of designer fashions.

In fact, due to their wealth of knowledge and breadth of experiences, well elders are in many respects the backbones of society. Retired business executives are invaluable members of corporate and agency boards of directors. And, as volunteer mentors to young entrepreneurs through governmental and corporate programs, many retirees put their knowledge and experience to work.

DECLINES IN FUNCTION AND HEALTH

Other older persons, particularly those over seventy-five, experience frailty, both physical and mental, and are susceptible to needing at least some assistance with their everyday activities. They may no longer be able to drive or use public transportation. With safety compromised, walking stairs can be too much of a challenge, the bathtub may leave them accident prone and an inability to remember whether they have paid a bill or deposited a check leaves them vulnerable for financial exploitation and scamming. For some of these people, especially those who live alone, a change of routine is called for.

Disabled individuals often need the assistance of others with their daily activities, and their independence and quality of life may be compromised. If unable to keep track of their medications and health regimens, these individuals often require sustained personal care at home either by family members, paid caregivers or both. Also available are community-based services such as adult day health centers, home-delivered meals and chore services or residential placement in a care facility, such as assisted living or a nursing home.

There is no way to predict whether changes in health will be sudden or gradual. Health problems come in all gradations, from mild to severe. These changes affect every aspect of life including emotions, relationships, finances and lifestyle. Chronic illnesses, such as heart disease, Parkinson's, arthritis and lung disease, may progress gradually, allowing for adaptation and planning. For those with sudden changes—a disabling accident, stroke or cancer—there is a "revolution" rather than an evolution, change for which there could be little or no preparation. These changes have a huge impact.

THE ADULT-CHILD CAREGIVER

Suddenly and unexpectedly thrust into the role of parent care, the adult child adds yet another dimension to their many roles. There are no job descriptions and few role models—and, most importantly, no timetables, as caregiving may actually go on for years. Gerontologists now speak of "the caregiving career," meaning that the nature, intensity and frequency of involvement changes over time according to the care recipient's changing physical, psychological and emotional states. Because caregiving is so widespread and can have adverse health effects, caregiving is fast becoming a public health and policy crisis and dilemma.

The adult-child caregiver may be from forty to eighty years old, spanning most of the age range dubbed "middle age" and beyond. Both men and women actively participate, but the "dutiful daughter or daughter-in-law" is doing most of the hands-on care. Women provide care to parents, parents-in-law, friends, spouses and neighbors. Not only do they provide hands-on health care, but they also serve as advocates and surrogate decision makers. While women spend 50 percent more time providing care than men, men also play a necessary role. Generally, it is the men who take care of home maintenance, such as fixing leaky faucets or repairing faulty locks, as well as overseeing financial and legal affairs. However, there are differences between cultures. In some Asian cultures, for example, it is the oldest son who is the primary caregiver; in others, it's the youngest.

WOMEN IN THE WORKFORCE

Women are a major part of the workforce. The majority are no longer at home, available to exclusively offer hands-on child and parent care. Rather, while attempting to secure a better life for their families, they may have demanding careers. Job duties are heaped upon already overscheduled lives. They are busier than ever, harried, multitasking and getting their ever-busy kids to activities. Like men, they are working longer and harder, and many families depend on two incomes. Caregiving poses financial challenges for women in the workforce, in terms of lost wages due to absenteeism or family leave, unattained promotions and enforced early retirement. Compelled to meet the pushes and pulls of their jobs as well as their children, their elders and themselves, middle-aged women, in particular, are caught in the sandwich, squeezed from both ends.

WHAT DOES IT MEAN TO BE A CAREGIVER?

A role that often comes unexpectedly, caregiving is physically, emotionally and economically challenging. Demanding our full attention, it can be overpowering. Fortunately, this does not last long. Having resiliency, we pull through. But, what exactly is it about caregiving that makes it so tough?

As a caregiver, we are forced to review our own lives and examine our relationships—past and present—with the older person, our spouse or significant other, siblings, children, grandchildren and friends and neighbors. It may cause us to examine our lifestyle, including our jobs and leisure activities and our own dreams and plans. After all, caregiving challenges are not occurring in a vacuum. The caregiving role may become a harbinger of our own vulnerabilities, causing anxiety about the future. It may remind us of past crises or life events, reawakening old conflicts with parents, siblings and other relatives. Conversely, it may help us to recall previously successful coping strategies.

Becoming a caregiver also forces us to look at our daily routines and behaviors. Can we become more available to our frail elder? How can we reallocate our time? Do we want to? How much time away will our spouses, children and bosses tolerate? Can we accept the unpredictability of caregiving? And how can we modify our behaviors so that we are not constantly venting our frustrations at the care recipient or innocent others?

Caregiving also causes us to test our own beliefs about aging, illness, dying, death and duty. It invites endless questions about our parents: Did we really think our parents would never change? Did we expect time to stand still? Did we believe that they would always be there for us, or at least, that they would be able to care for themselves forever? And, for perhaps the first time, it raises questions about ourselves: Are we afraid of who we are? What if we were to become our mother or our father? What if we were to develop heart disease, Alzheimer's or a stroke and become helpless or confused? What are our beliefs about death? Can we discuss with our parents how they really feel and what they want in terms of end-of-life care? Is this different from what we would want for ourselves? Would we be able to let go? How would we deal with their loss?

There is also a sense of duty. How guilty would we feel if we weren't there for them? This is particularly acute when facing the need to place a parent in an assisted living or a nursing home facility, often despite prior pleas like, "Promise me you'll never put me away?" And if you did promise, how guilty would you feel then?

It may be easy for you to be a model caregiver if your parents were so for you. But what if they weren't? This was true for Jake.

Jake: The Lion Who Turned into a Lamb

Jake, Ann's father, had been living alone and seemed perfectly capable. Oh, yes, he was getting old but "good genes" ran in the family. His parents had lived into their nineties, and he was heading in the same direction. Not that she gave it much thought, except that she, too, could live into old, old age. The youngest of three children, Ann was the only girl, with great space between the three, her mother referring to her birth as "the accident." Her father treated her as such, remarking frequently that if she had not been born, he and her mother could have traveled more, saved more, done more and that, if anything, she was a "burden." Despite this, she now lived a good life, had friends, male and female, and, as a single woman in her late forties, felt blessed with it all.

It seemed as if Dad became old overnight—no crises, no midnight calls and no brothers alerting her—just a series of changes: he now couldn't see too well, hear too well or walk too well, despite eyeglasses, a hearing aid and a cane. A nursing home was "out of the question," since he would not agree to it. There was only one thing he wanted and that was to come and live with Ann.

She told her closest friend, "Suddenly, he's sugar and spice. Where has he been the last forty-eighty years? No place, not for me, anyway. So now, he thinks he can tumble into my life and turn it upside down? No way." She continued, "I'm not going to wind up being his caregiver." Yet life often seems to have a plan all its own.

She saw that when she did visit her father, he was not only delighted to see her but dejected when she started to leave. He also offered a perspective on the past that he had not shown before. "Ann," he said, "I was never really there for you. What a fool I was. And look at you. You turned out to be a wonderful young woman. I never really knew you." Beginning to sob, he quickly wiped his tears away with an apology. Ann felt it to be real, and when she asked him again if he had considered living with either of his sons, he said that their wives may object, that she had a large apartment and that he really loved her very much and would like to get to know her before he died. Ann pushed aside her initial response of wanting her brothers to do their duty.

Instead, she very deliberately decided to become a family caregiver. She invited him to come live with her. Thereafter, she also managed to leave time for her job, her friends and leisure pursuits, cutting corners from what she had done in the past. Having chosen with full intent, she now saw her father in a new light. Age had gently rounded his edges. The lion had turned into a lamb; his true remorse touched Ann deeply. When, five years later, he died, she had held his hand at his bedside. As she told it, "I would not have missed that for the world."

Ann opened herself to new experiences and made conscious choices. All of this was transformative for her. Likewise, Jake did a little changing, too. The stereotype of "you can't teach an old dog new tricks" is just that—stereotype. Old age is not a steel container. Aging per se can be fluid, and even the steel container can have some holes through which light can enter. Jake saw the light and was able to move with it. The end result was positive not only for the father but for the daughter as well. While this was true for Ann and Jake, it is not necessarily so for all.

Mabel: The De Facto Care Recipient

Mabel has three children and four grandchildren and lives alone near two of her children. A severe diabetic, she requires close monitoring and supervision, especially around medications and meals. Her daughter, Laura, stops by early each morning on her way to work to measure mom's sugar, give her a shot and her other medications and cook breakfast. Her son, Robert, uses his lunch hour to bring her lunch and eat with her. Her other daughter, Juliana, takes care of dinner. Doctor visits are handled on a rotating basis, as are errands and household chores. Anxiety is democratically distributed among all the family members. But, ask Mabel about her situation, and she will tell you, "Everything is fine. I really don't need any help."

Some people with infirmities are steadfast in their denial that anything is wrong. They don't see, they don't hear and they don't feel that anything is wrong. Anyone who even mildly suggests that they need help is dismissed as anything from "nonsensical" to "mean." Don't confuse them with the facts, and don't inflict any help on them. Anything you offer will be considered an affront to them. You may see the contradictions between their demands for and acceptance of your help and their protestations that they don't need anything, but don't bother interpreting. Accept the fact that you are, indeed, the de facto caregiver.

Caregiving comes with challenges and complexities and often feels like a drag; however, it can also be a self-enlightening experience. Whether positive or negative, you are learning and preparing for your own aging. While being sandwiched would seem to imply that the situation is static, that sandwich can change. It can be understuffed or bulging. The bread can be thick or thin. Caregiving is a dynamic, fluid situation. Things change. The care recipient's needs change. Those around us change. We change. Even when things seem to stand still, they're changing. Getting a grip on your sandwich by breaking it into manageable bites can make it palatable or even tasty.

· 2 ·

Philosophies, Beliefs and Traits

$\mathcal{W}$e don't usually think about it, but everyone has a philosophy of life. The beliefs of the Greek philosophers, Socrates, Plato and Aristotle, became common knowledge as they spread the word. Jesus established his beliefs and a new religion formed around them. Moses discussed his beliefs with God, as he questioned whether or not he, Moses, could be a leader of the people God had chosen to go into a new land.

Now, you live by a set of principles called a theme. Some call it a mission, some call it a philosophy and others call it beliefs. These set you in motion and keep you there throughout your day and your life. You may be cynical (a belief), optimistic (a belief), religious (a belief), agnostic or atheist (both beliefs). But, a believer you are. Your elder is a believer too. And the interactions of your beliefs impact both your caregiving actions and your elder's care.

COMMON CAREGIVING BELIEFS

The following cases are examples of common beliefs found in the realm of caregiving that we have seen over and over again. They may include some of yours.

This first belief is that only families can provide care—children owe it to their parents. The parent took care of several children; a child can at least take care of one parent.

Francesca: The Selfless Caregiver

Francesca is a forty-year-old mental health professional who lives with her ailing mother. She is sweet and caring. The primary physician has recommended that her mother, now in her nineties, needs to be placed outside the home. Francesca says,

> I owe it to her to be there for her. I was a sickly child, the youngest of the six. She never deserted me. Why should I desert her now? Men? I'm really too tired to date. I get home late, have seen people all day, relieve the person who is there with Mom since Dad died ten years ago and just plop into bed. Weekends—well, I am just there. I'm family. Family is family.

Francesca has totally dedicated herself to her mother's care, not at her mother's request, but as a result of her belief system in full play.

While we may think only daughters are high on nurturance and selflessness, some sons are not far behind. Gordon was one of them.

Gordon: The Nurturing Son

> I know dad needs a nursing home. But, he won't last long there. It's the end of the line. They all go there to die. True, I checked out a few, but why would I want that for him? He was a great dad. He took me to ball games, bought me what I wanted, sent me—in fact, insisted—I go to college. I can't think of a better dad. Why would I do this to him now? My sister wants me to, but I won't give my consent.

His belief was that "nursing homes are for other people, but not my parent." No matter that there are some excellent ones, plus a variety of placement options to fit the needs of the person being placed, Gordon's belief is deeply ingrained and not to be disputed. Not to mention the fact that his dad has said to him, "Son, I think it's all too much for me—and for you and your sisters. Jenny, from next door, is in that new nursing home down the street, and her daughter told me she has friends there, the food is good and the staff is sweet. I think I could try it. If I don't like it, I could come home." But Gordon is adamant: "No, Dad, that's not for you."

A belief stays part of the person and cannot be dislodged unless you make a conscious effort. But, first you need to be aware of the belief.

Valentina: Cynical Daughter

Valentina had a similar belief, but another rationale. Since coming to the United States, she had been mugged once and had her home broken into. She became convinced that, in the United States, people steal more easily than in her country of origin. Both her parents were in wheelchairs in a small apartment, with one person taking care of them. On weekends, when Valentina was not working, either she or her brother became the caregiver and provided total care. They slept on the couch, with her turning her two young children over to their father for care. Her brother, single, stayed and slept where he could—often on the carpet near the parents' bed. Why not a placement? "People in nursing homes steal," they said. When asked how they know that, they looked as though you had asked them if the moon came out at night. Nothing would convince them otherwise. And so, in the case of prejudices, the facts do not fit the belief. But the latter wins out just the same.

Nancy: The Grateful Caregiver

While Gordon and Valentina faithfully stuck to their beliefs, Nancy found herself in a very different situation. For as long as she could remember, her mother, Willa, had impressed upon her the importance of family and the need for family care in old age. Nancy truly wanted to adhere to these wishes. However, one day she fell into a catastrophic situation that made her confront reality. Willa had gone to the hospital for a routine cardiac procedure and experienced a complication that led to irreversible damage, necessitating her being placed on a respirator. The physicians indicated that this would be permanent. One day she was fully functional; the next, she needed total care—and machines. Devastated, Nancy had to make a quick decision. Willa could not remain in the acute hospital indefinitely; rather, she would need to be placed in a nursing home. Much as she wanted to, Nancy was not able to provide home care. So, despite her reluctance, she was forced to find a ventilator bed in a long-term care facility. She did and was a faithful visitor. Willa lived in the facility for almost a year. Nancy felt that she received good care and said, "I tried my darnedest and have no regrets. Thank goodness, good care was available when my mother needed it. Staff members were absolutely angels. I don't know how they can do it day after day after day."

Roberta: The Reluctant Caregiver

Another popular belief is that "mother needs her independence." In the case of seventy-eighty-year-old Bertha, a widow who was diagnosed with middle-stage Alzheimer's disease, her daughter, Roberta, supported her wish to remain alone in her suburban home and drive her car, despite warnings from neighbors and friends about her lack of safety.

Having her daily routine, she never went far from home, and the family, thus, played down her vulnerability. One day, while she was driving home from church, she hit another car and just kept on going. A policeman happened to be riding by. Stopping her, he confiscated the car and called Roberta to come and get her. Additionally, the police reported the accident to the insurance company and informed Motor Vehicles of her apparent impairment.

Roberta was now faced with having to rethink Mom's independence. In an initial consultation with a professional, she said, "I can't take the car away from Mom. She'll die." Roberta similarly resisted getting home help for mom because, "Mom needs her privacy." Sometimes we get blinded by our own beliefs, as well intentioned as they may be. In this situation, Bertha's vulnerabilities were brought to light by her automobile accident.

BALANCING INDEPENDENCE AND DEPENDENCE

Sooner or later, addressing vulnerabilities is a necessity. The Greeks had it right when they insisted on the balanced life being the healthy life. Eating is fine if you don't overeat—or undereat. The same goes for exercise—or for anything. Proportion and balance promote healthy living. So, if independence is necessary—and it is—so is dependence. A person having difficulty walking—when streets are slippery, with new snow having fallen—is foolish not to ask for help to cross the street. The balanced person asks while one who is too ashamed to ask becomes vulnerable to falling, with possible drastic results. So, dependence is not always a bad thing, especially when a little bit of assistance may actually preserve a life.

Another familiar belief is, "I must leave something for the kids. Otherwise, what was the point to it all?"

Gail: My Money Is My Legacy

Gail, the primary caregiver for her husband with Parkinson's disease, has just been diagnosed with breast cancer and has decided to begin radiation and chemotherapy treatments. Adamant about the importance of family, having been a devoted wife, mother and grandmother and known as a giving person, she insists that she's strong and otherwise healthy and will be able to care for her husband as well as herself without additional help. After all,

> my money is my legacy. I need to save it for my children and grandchildren. You know how much college costs each year? Education is so expensive, and even successful parents cannot meet the extraordinary costs without help. If they use loans, the kids will be in debt forever. What good are grandparents if we can't help our kids? What did we work and save for?

Not wanting to dig into her vast savings, Gail's expectation was that her adult children would drop everything and provide total care, despite their heavy everyday responsibilities that included professional careers and young children.

Inheritance is the transfer of wealth between generations. Meaning different things to different people, it could be the family home, art, antiques, jewelry, stocks, bonds or currency. With Gail, the intent was to be remembered, to leave a legacy, footsteps that can be walked in and memories that can be held onto. Alive, we are visible. Afterward, no matter what our beliefs are about death, we want to be a part of the people we leave behind.

PREFERENCES

If beliefs are the printouts that guide you through your day, your preferences further define your quality of life. Not random, they are an intrinsic part of you. You know your preferences and show them to the world: where you live, how you dress, what vacations you choose to take, what books you read, what you eat, your television viewing, the friends you choose, your career path, the choices for intimacy and your lifestyle are all preferences. In this world swamped with options, you have made conscious choices and put your stamp on them. Even when you make a change in your choices, it is still your choice. For older people, their preferences have been around for decades.

Lila: A Conscious Lifestyle Change

Lila always resisted being a "snowbird," going down south for the winter, feeling, "I can't stand being surrounded by so many older people, and what's wrong with buying boots, wearing a warm coat and walking in the glorious snow, anyway?" And then, she slipped on the ice and fractured a hip. After recuperation, she turned into a snowbird. She had made a choice. Another option would have been to remain up north and stay inside during cold, icy weather, and if the occasion arose when she absolutely had to go out, to rely on her husband to escort her.

Now what about you? You also have your preferences. While your preferences have value, they are yours. Express them, but don't impose them on others. As a caregiver, focus on the preferences of the elder. Now that Lila's preference has been put into action, think about how you can work with it: How often can you fly down south to see her? How long can you stay? What about phone calls, e-mails and other means of staying in touch?

Don: The Widower Who Remarries

One of the most contentious preferences is when a widowed parent chooses to remarry. Don, at seventy-two, was youthful looking and vigorous. He and

Kelly had been married for forty-five years when, after a short, painful illness, she passed away. Their two daughters and son were all married with children. Don had a good job, substantial savings and a pension. After a little more than a year, he met Rebecca at a friend's dinner party. Attractive and energetic, Rebecca, who had never been married, said, "Don is my first true love. It's taken me a long time, but I'm finally there."

The children were horrified. "How could you do this to us? It's not that we don't like Rebecca, but this is so unlike you. You are such a considerate and careful person. Do you really know what you're doing? We're worried about you." Don listened, but he went ahead with his plan. Having been a person who truly knew what he wanted, he tuned into his inner voice and went ahead. He said to his children, "Listen, Mom was very, very special, and I dearly loved her. Rebecca is another person, her own. And I love her for who she is. It is my choice and I hope you will respect it. Remember, I will love all of you just as I always have and the memory of your mother as well."

REMARRIAGE

Children may approve in principle of the idea of remarriage for a parent but find it appalling when it actually is about to happen, as in the case of Don. Expressed fears include the following: "She's after your money (and, therefore, our inheritance). You don't know her well enough. She may have different interests. You don't know how healthy she is. And we may have to wind up taking care of both of you." Underlying all of this is the real reason: he is being disloyal to your mother. Another woman is taking her place in bed, using her things, setting the table with her best silverware and, all in all, just taking over. While, in the case of Don, there were no stepchildren, he had his own children to contend with. Were there stepchildren and grandchildren, this may have been compounded by a clash of values, preferences, jealousies and competition for time and attention: "With whom will you spend Christmas now?"

PERSONALITY TRAITS

Both beliefs and preferences are part of your total personality. Your beliefs are your philosophy of life translated into action. Your preferences are the unique choices you make based upon these beliefs. All of these preferences and beliefs were right there from the beginning. It used to be thought that you were born as a blank slate, and anyone and everything that happened to you became firmly implanted, to remain there for the rest of your life. Your parents said this and that, your siblings were kind or unkind and so forth, as if it struck you as a thunderbolt and formed an imprint that stayed forever—not so.

New research says that you are born with certain personality traits, there from day one and lasting forever. As against everything we had been told until then, the parental impact is small, 10 percent or less. How you respond to everything is quite distinct from how your siblings respond. Your genetic inheritance accounts for 40 to 50 percent of your personality. Your unique, very individual response makes up the balance of who you are. Thus, in a family of five, with parents' responding similarly to all five, your unique response is yours alone, which is why attuned parents may say, "Each of my children is different." These findings have been validated by the most recent social science studies of identical twins that were reared apart and, when discovered decades later, were found to have traits and behaviors that were very similar in nature.

How does this affect you as an adult? How does it affect you in your role as a caregiver? You will respond to your parents based upon your particular traits. Likewise, they will respond to you. Twelve have been identified.

NEED FOR COMPANIONSHIP

You showed this at birth. As a baby, you could not tolerate maternal separation. You disliked being left alone in your crib even for a short time. When it was time to enter nursery school or kindergarten, you cried when Mommy left. Called "separation anxiety," you were uneasy when your parent left. Now, here you are, thirty, forty or fifty years later, and that trait is still there. You like and need closeness. Sharon says, "Here I am, a fifty-two-year-old woman. My mother is a widow, eighty-five and frail but not unusually so. We have someone in the house with her, but all I do is think of her dying, and I feel that old hysterical feeling coming over me."

Older adults with this trait have the same need for closeness. After her husband died, Martha could not bear to stay alone in her apartment at night. She arranged to have her niece come to sleep in her apartment every night. After a while, she moved in with her married daughter. Several years later, when she entered a nursing home, she chose to have a shared suite because she wanted the company of a roommate. Traits are embedded.

While many older adults live alone, particularly women since they generally outlive men, this may not be their situation of choice. Loneliness and isolation can set in, thus increasing their vulnerabilities—both physical and mental.

IDEALISM

Idealism is an energizing trait that colors everything we do. The idealist thinks of people as basically honest, good and trustworthy. This mindset encompasses aspects of religion, spirituality, mysticism, ethics and morality. Children who display this trait are particularly compassionate, showing concern for others at an early age. A friend cries and they comfort them. Idealists are optimists, who say the world is good and I am good, perform heroic acts and trust in the goodness of others.

SUBJECTIVE WELL-BEING

Subjective well-being has to do with how you feel about yourself. Basically, you are an optimist or a pessimist. If you are an optimist, you will consistently see the glass of water as half full. As we grow older, we acquire an internal thermostat so that we continually check our feelings as to how we respond to the daily ups and downs of life along with major experiences, whether joyful or not so wonderful. This viewpoint stays with us for all of our life.

Charlene: The Eternal Optimist

Seventy-year-old Charlene went to a shopping mall. When she got home, she realized that she had left her wallet at the coffee bar. Though it did not contain much money, it had her identification, health insurance cards, driver's license and other essentials. She called a couple of her friends and mentioned this in passing. At that point, everybody insisted that she immediately put a "stop" on everything and wondered why she was not more upset and proactive. Charlene, in her calm voice, told them that she believed that some "good soul would find it and come through for me." Her friends were skeptical at best, but she followed her gut and waited. Within two days, a call came from a young college student who had found the wallet and wanted to return it to her in person. She did, and when offered a small reward, said, "No, I was glad to do this and am happy that I found it." Charlene remains the eternal optimist.

The opposite is the trait of cynicism, feeling and expressing the idea that most people are selfish, uncaring and not to be trusted. Going back to our example of Valentina, who, as you may remember, felt that people working in nursing homes steal—her trait was that of cynicism. This trait has caused her to take actions that have not only deprived her parents of the best available quality of care, but also have severely impacted her quality of life and that of her brother.

EMOTIONAL INTENSITY

While we all have a range of emotions, some of us are intense and some of us, less so. Gordon, if you recall, was the son who, despite his father's desire to "try a nursing home," was relentless in his refusal. His emotional intensity was high. This would be true of him as a baby—he would laugh, cry and react strongly to everything and everyone, while other babies would be more placid. Now, an adult, when dad even mentions trying a nursing home, he reacts with the same powerful strength of feeling that is his endowment. Here, his innate trait plays itself, in opposition to his father's, who feels quite differently. He wants to try a nursing home, where he believes he will be comfortable.

Not to be treated as a silent partner, his wishes need to be listened to and accommodated. Contrary to popular myths, most elders retain their intellectual faculties and are not to be dismissed as incompetent. They can and should be active participants in care decision-making. After all, it's their life.

SPONTANEITY

Kate was eighty when she went to live with her daughter, Yvonne, who had invited her. Her friends warned Kate against this: "You'll never be happy there. The grandkids will be noisy and you won't be able to follow your routine." But, spontaneous Kate disregarded these drawbacks. If we could know her as a baby, she would be the one to coo and gurgle with pleasure when you dangled a new toy in front of her. If we followed her through high school, she would be the risk-taker and, into adulthood, the entrepreneur. That did not change. She moved into her daughter's home, welcomed the novelty and lived there until she passed away.

This flexibility exists despite the stereotypes of older people as rigid, inflexible, unwilling to take challenges, unable to change and too old to learn. Obviously, this was not Kate. And, as you may suspect, she did not take anyone else's advice but her own.

Spontaneity is highly relevant and valuable to caregivers. Care recipients' needs fluctuate, and plans, strategies and services may have to take a new turn every now and then. You were not given a job description when you assumed this role, and you may not have had any role models. Sometimes, you have to improvise as you go along. "Go with the flow" is a helpful mantra for caregivers.

LIBIDO

Libido, or sexuality, is another of the twelve traits. The family caregiver may be higher or lower on libido, prioritizing how much time they spend with their spouse or significant other, accordingly. Realistically, caregiving may cut into family time and also time alone with one's partner.

On the other hand, having a care recipient who is high on libido and low on appropriate impulse control can be embarrassing and even humiliating for the caregiver. Remember Uncle Lenny and his niece, Rhonda? In Rhonda's presence, he told one of the nurses, "My friend had a beautiful ass, not like your skinny one." At least he didn't try to pinch her this time. Truth is that older people have sexual impulses. When appropriately carried out, sexual activity can be as enjoyable and pleasurable as for any younger person, despite the myths about aging robbing older people of their sexuality. What is lacking sometimes is the opportunity, especially for the older woman. The ratio of males to females over sixty decreases with each decade; however, the creative older woman often finds her man.

NURTURANCE

Another of the twelve traits is nurturance, on which caregivers may be high or low. Francesca, whom we have met and is totally dedicated to her mother, is the supernurturant woman. As a baby, she would become upset if she saw someone in distress. That would include animals as well. She chose a profession in which she exercises her compassion. Francesca is a social worker—a good match.

Nurturance is a good thing when not carried to extremes. It is an enveloping trait, without which none of us could have survived. A child who is not basically nurtured leads a detached life, being unaware of compassion for or attachment to other people and separateness from themselves. People who become caregivers discover and put to use their warm and sweet nurturing traits. Using this quality, we derive joy and fill our purpose in helping others. While it affects the individual, it also affects the family by bringing all closer together.

EXTROVERSION

The extroverted infant thrives on social attention. As "people people," they stay that way. Al is a typical example, telling us about his mom: "She needs to get out more. I think she is depressed. I worry. Staying home by herself, she just takes solitary walks. No people, no stimulation, nothing. Oh, yes, she reads a lot. But, you know, she needs people. I mean, everyone has friends, goes to meetings, church and the movies. It's not good to just be by yourself." When asked how she was before his father died, he said, "Well, now that I think about it, she read and liked to be alone. She and dad got along okay, but I still think she preferred her own company." He laughed. "I guess I'm just feeling that I could not do that. So, how could she?" Al's comments reveal his trait of extroversion.

Being shy and quiet is not necessarily negative. If your sense of self is secure, you may not need or want many people around you. This is contrary to the fearful person who is shy and quiet, due to fear of criticism or the lacking of social skills for interaction. Typical of the latter is Tom, who now at the age of eighty-two is aware of his developing dementia. He says, "My wife insists that I go with her to all social events. But I feel like the silent partner. I never get to say what I want. All I hear is chatter around me, and by the time I can get the words out, somebody has already said it. Like a turtle, I retreat back into my shell."

AESTHETICISM

"Where there is music, there can be no evil," wrote Cervantes more than three hundred years ago in Don Quixote. For those who share the trait of Aestheticism, music, art and all of nature's beauty are high on their list of what life is all about. The saying, "Song is the language of the angels" would be a favorite of theirs. For those with this trait, from the moment they leave the womb, they react hungrily to intense aesthetic stimulation—color and sound. By early childhood, they dance, sing or draw, and many show obvious talent in one or more of these areas. As adults, they frequent movies, concerts, art exhibits, opera, ballets and plays. If your aging parent is high on this quality, know that their preference would be an environment that reflects this trait.

ACTIVITY LEVEL

Activity level affects you, the caregiver. You are either high or low. As a baby, you either slept a little or a lot. If you had a high activity level, getting you to bed was a chore. You were just always on the go—and never changed. In the playground, you went on and on, with endless energy, exhausting everyone around you, but not yourself. You seemed indefatigable and stayed that way. So, now that you have to care for another, remember who you are, and take on chores accordingly.

The activity level of the care recipient will also impact your caregiving experience. If the recipient wants to be constantly busy and is thus "high maintenance," know this when you make plans. If your care recipient doesn't sleep much at night, and you have a job to get to in the morning, you will have to find a way to address your sleep deprivation—perhaps a night shift of help. The trick here is to stay in sync with your trait and that of the care recipient. Know the difference. Overdoing is overkill, and burn-out will not be far behind. Modulate your activity level.

MATERIALISM

"I'm a thing person," says the materialist. Possessions, objects that can be seen, felt, worn and, possibly, stored away, are their passion. While materialism itself is not a bad trait, excesses can be. People who are excessive on this trait may be hoarders, unwilling to share anything that they have accumulated, including monies, clothes, objects or gains anticipated through inheritance. Such was the case with Ursula. Ursula's mother-in-law, a financially secure woman, was now terminally ill. While her husband's sisters wanted to place Mom in a comfortable, well-regarded nursing-care facility, Ursula was vehement in her protestations. "My mother-in-law doesn't need it. It's a waste of money. Her house is beautiful. She has all she needs. How long is she going to live anyway, so what's the point? Wasted money is wasted money." Appalled at Ursula's greed, the family overruled her and proceeded with placement.

Practically speaking, there may be economic constraints to consider. Long-term care is expensive, and at-home care can be as costly or even more so. In Ursula's case, her opposition to placement was borne out of greed rather than consideration of the patient's care needs and economic circumstances.

Unlike Ursula, most families show generosity when it comes to caregiving, sacrificing themselves and often their own resources. No matter how you look at it, caregiving is expensive. What's at stake here is the possibility of time lost on your job, missed promotions, lack of attention to your professional duties, missed benefits, greatly increased stress and the neglect of your own personal needs.

INTELLECTUALISM

The trait of intellectualism has a focus on ideas. If your aging person is, what is termed, an "egghead" and always was, they need an environment that plays to that. For them, "getting high on ideas" has been and will remain the ideal. Books, philosophies and intellectual stimulation of all kinds are, for them, what life is all about. Take your cues from this. However, if you're the "egghead" and words replace action, then you have to know this, too. Intellectualism can be a positive and wonderful inborn trait, but it can also be an obstacle to action. This is not to say that intellectuals are to be discounted; in fact, they are an important group in our society. Caregivers may read, research and think about problems— all to the good. However, there comes a point where you have to reach a conclusion and take action. If you just stay with the ideas, nobody benefits.

Joyce: The Analyzer

Joyce, intellectually gifted, has a doctorate in philosophy and is a professor of ethics at a local college. An only child, she is the caregiver for her mom, Eleanor, a long-time widow, who lives alone in a majestic home in a desirable neighborhood. Eleanor has become more and more forgetful and isolated, even from her immediate neighbors. Joyce visits weekly and on holidays and occasionally escorts her to the hairdresser or to medical appointments. With her house becoming more and more cluttered, Joyce is taking care of the bills, as she meticulously hunts for them. Aware of her mother's increasing decline, she rationalizes that, despite all appearances, her mother is in a secure house in a safe neighborhood and is living comfortably.

On one of her visits, Joyce finds her mother with an obvious problem with her arm, yet unaware of her injury. A trip to the Emergency Room reveals a fracture. Thankful that Eleanor doesn't need surgery, Joyce hires a home health aide to live with her temporarily. The hospital social worker had suggested that, at this point and most likely in the future, the mother would require more care and supervision. But, now that she has hired a temporary aide, the daughter does not feel an urgency to do anything more.

Two weeks later, in the presence of the home health aide, Eleanor fell and there was another trip to the Emergency Room. This time, it's a hairline fracture of the ankle. Again, Joyce was thankful that no surgery was required. Eleanor needed to stay off her feet temporarily, and Joyce would help by reading aloud to her the great classics that she knew so well. "This will make her feel so much better. It does for me. I know it will for her, too. She'll forget all about her pain."

It was now strongly suggested to Joyce that she consider an alternative living arrangement for Eleanor. Consider it she did—consider and consider. And read and research she did, too. Dropping by a few eldercare places, she decided that none were good enough. "My mother would never be happy here. This is not for her. There's no intellectual stimulation going on. These people are not on her level. It's also not especially convenient for me to visit."

In the meantime, the clutter grew, the isolation became more intense and Eleanor's vulnerability increased substantially. Joyce did not want to upset her mother by insisting that she move to an Assisted Living Facility. She loved her mother and believed that she was taking good care of her, since it was "only age that was creeping up on her." Although Joyce believed that the changes that were happening to Eleanor were "a normal part of aging," she accepted the idea that, indeed, her mother needed some changes to be made. Yet, the idea stayed an idea, and Joyce could not and did not do anything about it.

AGING: GROWTH, CHALLENGE, AND CHANGE

Affecting the caregiving process are your underlying beliefs about aging, illness, death and dying. Aging is a dynamic process that brings with it growth, challenge and change. Aging begins at birth. We go from infancy to childhood, adolescence, young adulthood, middle age, old age and, as is now evident, old, old age. Over time, skills and roles change, as do the situations around us.

What about challenge? Challenge is not necessarily always your choice, but it does come in the form of biological changes, which, while intrinsic to aging, are not necessarily detriments. You may still be doing yoga but may have to accommodate to bodily changes in terms of the positions you can now perform. It may take more time to run a marathon, but you do finish. All older people are not sick and infirm, but a little compromise may go a long way.

The real challenge is that while aging is a normative process, there are some diseases that are more common with increasing age. Examples are high blood pressure, heart disease, arthritis, cancer and Alzheimer's. These conditions may be mild, moderate or severe, acute or chronic. Although some are controllable by lifestyle changes, medications and alternative therapies, they may be life-altering. Others can be disabling enough to necessitate hands-on assistance, ranging from minimal help to total care. In some cases, people become dependent even though they did not want to. This has to be accepted and respected.

PAIN

Your beliefs and your traits deeply affect how you care for your elder. For example, if you believe that suffering is a normal part of aging, you may, in turn, dismiss and resent what you see as their complaining and dependence. Unfortunately, this is all too true for health professionals, along with our general society. Comments such as "What do you expect at your age?" are common.

Given the negative stereotypes about aging, pain tends to be underrecognized, undertreated and dismissed. The fact is, pain is pain at any age, as is suffering. The experience of pain reflects a strong mind-body connection. Pain may affect sleep, mood, appetite, energy level, body image and function and may engender feelings of increased stress, helplessness, hopelessness and loss of control.

Listen to what your care recipient is telling you, and observe his or her body language. Pain may affect multiple parts of the body simultaneously. Don't be flip about the details. Try to understand what the symptoms are telling you, and do something about them: Pain management is available. Seek it out.

END-OF-LIFE CARE

Death has many faces. If you believe that there is life after death, you look at death as a stepping stone into a better and purer world. If you see death as the final end, that is another way to look at life. Each has its own validity. Again, your beliefs will impact your role as a caregiver. Your beliefs are yours.

In the caregiving situation, you need to know the beliefs of the care recipient on this issue. Only then can their end-of-life care be planned appropriately. Where there has been no talk about this and discussion is no longer possible, a search for some written documents, such as a Health-Care Proxy, Living Will or Durable Power of Attorney, needs to be done. If there is no written documentation, act in your loved one's behalf, doing what you feel they would have wanted.

There has been increasing attention to end-of-life care options: comfort care, palliative care and hospice are choices available in the home, in assisted living or in nursing facilities. Hospice patients are cared for by a multidisciplinary team, which may include nurses, social workers, physicians, psychologists and clergy. You, as family, are an integral part of this team. The issue is care versus cure, fostering quality of life as opposed to quantity. For example, if someone has terminal cancer and hospice is chosen, aggressive therapies such as chemotherapy or surgery will be stopped, and the patient will receive pain management, along with nursing care, personal care and family and patient bereavement counseling.

Accepting the imminence of death is more than difficult. Caregivers, who have valiantly struggled with their relative, have to face the realities of this end-of-life experience and refocus their efforts. We all make conscious choices about how we want to live—and how we want to die. Caregivers and care recipients may have entirely different views on the subject. These need to be accepted without judgment.

In the difficult situation you are in as part of the "sandwich generation," awareness of your philosophy, beliefs and traits as well as those of your care recipient can offer you much. "What is good? What is the right thing to do? How about mistakes—can they be rectified?" Let your beliefs be your guide.

• *3* •

A Kaleidoscope of Families: Tied and Untied

Children begin by loving their parents: as they grow older they like them; later they judge them; sometimes they forgive them.

—Oscar Wilde in Dorian Gray

PARENTS AND CHILDREN

*W*hen parents have children and you ask them, "Which child is your favorite," there are vehement protestations: "I have no favorites. I love them all equally." While parents may distribute love equally like a warm blanket that protects them from the cold, liking is another story. One most likes the child who is closest to the parent in style. The reason is simple: they are easy to be with for that parent. On the opposite end of the scale is a child who is difficult.

> He was always just a pain. I kept getting called to school all the time. It was embarrassing. And to make it worse, I was on the advisory council of the parents' association. And as I would stand up to speak, I could see everyone's eyes on me. I knew what they were thinking and could see compassion in their eyes. Inwardly, I could feel myself shrinking. He's no different now. I hear it all from his wife as she sometimes says, "Didn't you teach him anything, Mom?" At that point, I shrug my shoulders and say, "It's your turn, honey; now you do your part."

Another mother says,

> She was always different. I could never understand her. Of my four daughters, this one was dropped from an alien planet into the wrong baby basket,

27

I think. She was not a bad kid—just different. She was always uppity. She says, "Mom, I'm just not going to hang out with them. All they talk about is boys and clothes. They never read. All they do is sit and watch television and call each other, saying nothing. I don't answer because I have nothing to say to them. I think about college. They're worried about their next date." And where does she want to go? You guessed it. The three top colleges, of course. And who will pay for it all? She thinks her grades will get her a scholarship. Then, she'll surely be way above us.

These differences do not necessarily change over time. The kid who was wracking up misdemeanors is still up to his old tricks. And the future professor is just that, teaching Renaissance literature about which the parents have not a clue.

Linda was not particularly beautiful, but in the eyes of her parents, she was Cleopatra. Although small and slim, they saw her as a Venus. She could do no wrong. At fourteen, she tried lipstick. Her father looked at her: "Linda, you don't need lipstick. You look beautiful without it. I know it was not your idea, but your new friend's. She is not for you." "No, Dad, it was my idea, really. She didn't want to, but I thought we should try it." Dad smiled at her, "Honey, you can't fool me." And, so it was with her all her life. They thought she was absolutely perfect.

ADULT CHILDREN AND PARENTS

Let's fast-forward forty years. Where are mother and dad with the difficult son, now? Like many older adults, they have a chronic ailment or two but, uncomplaining, manage their lives quite successfully. While they don't need personal care, they do need some "doing" some of the time. "Brian, the painters were here. Could you come and rehang the pictures?" "Sure, Mom, I'll be there." But the days go by, and he does not come. Then, he finally does. Going in, he asks for some hooks. They look at him, "What hooks?" He says, "I thought you had some. I didn't bring any." The paintings remained on the floor until they called a neighbor who came and hung them.

And where are the parents of the "uppity" daughter? Mom died and dad is alone. He retired a few years ago from his job as a mason and now plays cards and hangs out with his buddies at the union hall. His daughters take turns visiting. When the professor comes, there's a lecture to follow: "Dad, I know you're making it now by yourself, but I'm worried about your future. I don't think you have enough intellectual stimulation. You might look at the retirement community near me. They have professional staff, talks, activities and entertainment, all in a beautiful setting. You really deserve better than what you've settled for." Dad responds, "I like it the way it is, and I plan to stay here." And so it was.

FAMILIES: HARMONY OR DISCORD

While some families have bumps in the road, some are as smooth as freshly paved asphalt. The Campbells were such a family. High school sweethearts, Stewart and Eva met, fell in love and married. Each seemed like a twin to the other; they completed each other's sentences. Mirroring each other, their love seemed a Hollywood story. When each of their three daughters and three sons were born, the love was shared and there seemed enough for everyone. Most of all, each child was treated as an individual and respected for their unique talents. When one son showed natural ability for sports and wanted to become a sports writer, he was encouraged to do so. Twenty years later, when everyone knew his name, his parents were not surprised and accepted it with both modesty and pride. When their daughter, Rowena, took ballet lessons and said she wanted to dance, everyone said, "But you're fat; you'll have to lose some weight." But neither Rowena nor her parents were discouraged. Some twenty years later, she was actually a member of a known ballet company. When friends came along with her parents to see her and asked which one she is, her mother said, "The fat one. Look at how graceful she is." The other children went off in their own directions, each given their parents' blessings.

Aging was a series of smooth passages for Stewart and Eva. Once the children were married, they chose to move to smaller quarters in a nearby "active adult" community that had a golf course, a clubhouse and a very active social environment. Stewart loved to play golf. Eva loved bridge, canasta and socializing. Both loved to travel overseas, and spent time and money bringing back gifts for all the grandchildren, as well as showing them photos of the places they had visited. The family aged as a symphony, with all of its members in harmony.

No unforeseen events took place until one morning when Stewart failed to wake up. No prior sign of illness, the cause of death was determined to be a massive heart attack. In shock, Eva asked her adult children "to let her be" until she could recover "and become my old self." With the usual respect accorded her, they did so.

Two years later, Eva called a family conference with her children, their spouses and the older grandchildren. She announced that she had rethought her life and decided that she should no longer remain by herself. She wanted to go and live with one of the children, whoever would find it most convenient, saying, with a laugh, "I love you all." After a short discussion, everyone agreed that it would be best for Eva to go to live with her middle daughter. Smooth sailing once again.

While we hear a lot about dysfunctional families and the angst that families go through around parent care, the truth is that many are functional and meet the challenges. These are not sensational stories featured on the evening news, but they do exist and are, in fact, a majority.

SIBLINGS

Family history may repeat itself. Old relationships either blossom or fester. Whatever wasn't solved early on is sure to rear its graying head as the years go by. Children come into this world with their traits, and parents make their choices. Competition may be set up from the get-go. The older child may be given responsibilities not in keeping with their chronological age. As he or she exclaims, "Everyone else is always off the hook, except me." A son who has been shunted aside may take a back seat in life, feeling that he's not worth much and can't please anybody; so why try? Children who have been given a great deal of responsibility may feel burdened but keep their anger to themselves, feeling, "Why am I always the one to do everything?" Children who are controlling and have their parents where they want them are seen by the others as arrogant, self-centered, bossy, mean and to be resisted at every step. Overly solicitous children may in their overt behavior be seeking attention, the underlying cry being, "Look at me, someone. Am I not worth something? Will anyone ever take notice?" Favorites may remain the favorite all of their life to the envy and outrage of the siblings.

Patty: The Responsible Daughter Who Is Left to Do Everything

Patty was the oldest daughter. At five, she was sent to the corner store, her mother secure that she would come back with the right food and the correct change. Patty, "the super daughter," did just that. On the way, she noticed all her friends playing, and when they asked her to come and play with them, she said, "My mommy sent me shopping. I can't." Inwardly, she was disappointed that she could not play when she wanted to. Away at college, she, one of four siblings, was called one night and told that there was an emergency and she had to come home. Her mother had fallen and hurt her back, and it was Patty she wanted with her for comfort. As it turned out, the injury was not severe. But this was part of a lifelong pattern of "Patty can do it." And Patty did.

Thirty years later, her mother decided to move and chose to live around the corner from Patty. "This way, my daughter is nearby and can drive me around. I'm too old to drive now, but she's not." Not considered was that Patty had a husband, her own teenage children and a teaching job. Her father passed on quickly after the move, and Patty was subjected to her mother's every whim. When she asked her siblings to help, the recurring theme was "No way, I can't manage what I'm doing already." When she responded with, "How come I can?" they countered with, "You always did, so why not continue now?"

Eventually, mother became ill and in need of a nursing home. Patty was her only consistent visitor. The others visited sporadically and stayed for only a short time. When her mother died, Patty made all the arrangements and had to contend with the disarray left behind in the mother's house. Ironically, the estate was left equally divided among all of the siblings. While everyone expected Patty to be outraged by this, she took it in stride. Her true feelings were kept to herself, her "public face" at ease. With her mother's death, would the family relationships change?

MELLOWING

Mellowing generally is associated with objects such as wine, cheese and beef. But individuals also mellow. They get gentler with age and the feistiness softens. Families, too, as a system, can mellow. Now that Patty's mother is no longer around and in control of her, with fierce repercussions for the family, the system has lost its volcanic intensity.

Patty could now use her energies to try to restore more positive sibling relationships. This does not happen overnight. Much as she had been ousted previously from her siblings' circle, she now had to work herself back in. She did this by following some of her former behaviors. For example, as a skilled teacher, she offered to tutor some of her nieces and nephews. This was received with great appreciation and served as a new gateway into their circle. A talented pianist, she started to entertain at family gatherings. The mellowing took time.

Charlotte: The Dutiful Daughter

Aging parents can become pawns in the competitive game called family relationships, where power becomes the theme. Charlotte is the fourth daughter of six children, three sons and three daughters, an evenness not to be replicated in the family system. She lives at home with her frail, dependent parents, having returned by choice when she perceived they needed her. Four of the siblings reside within twenty minutes of the parental home and the other a short plane trip away. Fragmented, the family has multiple splits, none of which seem to ever come together. For example, on holidays, most do their own thing, while Charlotte and her parents do nothing special. Anger is never overtly expressed, nor is any other emotion. Communication is almost nonexistent within this family structure, although it may exist within each family constellation by itself.

If we go beneath the surface, something more than old rivalries is going on. The father was dependent on drugs and alcohol for most of his life, and it had an enormous impact on his family, shame and humiliation being the least of it. The mother, though showing the face of the all-American family, pretended that nothing had ever happened. In the face of this pretense, one son became mentally ill and one daughter developed an addiction. Though seemingly more than just bright, none of them ever reached their professional potential.

Charlotte carried the full burden of her parents' care, relieving her siblings of all responsibility; yet they were deeply resentful of her. There was even the intimation that she, despite looks to the contrary, was a freeloader. In reality, Charlotte just did what she did out of a sense of duty. With time, the relationships, as poor as they had been, sank even lower.

Age did not treat them kindly, nor did they treat age kindly. At least in this, there was agreement. The likelihood of mellowing did not exist. After the death of both parents, the spokes of the wheel flew apart in different directions and stayed that way. If there was one person that was at peace, it was Charlotte. She had done what she had to do. To her, that's what life was all about.

DIFFERENT FAMILY CONFIGURATIONS

Families are no longer Mom, Dad, Dick, Jane and Spot, the dog. With half of marriages ending in divorce, there's been an untying and retying of family configurations. Not the least of this are single parents, who head their own households. Going back to our former story about Patty, imagine if she took on parent-care responsibilities as she did, on top of her being a single mother and full-time breadwinner. Impossible, you say, but not implausible. In fact, single parents do get stuck in the intergenerational sandwich, too.

Grace: The Deferring Daughter

Grace, a thirty-year-old administrative assistant and mother of two, lives in a comfortable home with her sixty-year-old mother. When her health became precarious, the mother was hospitalized. After her acute treatment, she was transferred to a nursing home for rehabilitation. Never having been meek, the mother continued her dominant style, using the telephone as her management tool. Whatever she wanted or needed, she picked up the phone and gave orders to her daughter. Ever compliant, Grace blindly deferred to her mother's wishes. Over time, the wishes progressively became more unreasonable. And when Grace didn't respond immediately, the mother would call others with the same demands, making Grace feel guilty for not being responsive enough.

It took others to remind her that she has a full-time job, two children and a sick mother, who, at times, breaks the boundaries of reasonableness. As one friend said to her, "Grace, listen, you're like the jelly in the peanut butter sandwich, oozing and overflowing. You've got to be more like the peanut butter. Toughen up. Stick." For Grace, this presents a formidable challenge, but she's working on it.

WHEN THE BLENDED FAMILY UNBLENDS

Muriel and Dave seemed to do very well, although their personality styles were not exactly the same. It was a second marriage for both. Dave was a successful businessman, and money was freely spent for household help, cars, a boat and trips abroad. They were socially active and had a large circle of friends. Both sets of children seemed to get along, and family holidays were jointly spent. Life had many rainbows, but then came the storm.

Dave collapsed one day of a heart attack, for which he was hospitalized. Major surgery quickly followed, and he was able to go home. The outcome was not as positive as they had hoped for, and Muriel was told that he would need constant care, with her supervising and coordinating it all. Now, feeling trapped, she thought, as much as it produced guilt in her, "I didn't count on this. Basically, I can't do it. I have to take care of myself. He has kids. They can pitch in now. I took care of one husband when I was younger and do not want a replay. Enough is enough."

Muriel felt strongly that Dave's kids were not off the hook just because she was there. She called a family meeting and insisted that he go to live with one of his children. They obliged. Fortunately, there was no quarrel over finances or possessions. Predictably, there were no more joint family holidays. A blender blends only that which can be blended.

THE GAY FAMILY

Brenda and Alexandra were drawn to each other in college and soon realized that their relationship was more than a friendship. Secretive for a long time, they eventually decided to come out. That meant that they could tell their friends, but what about their parents? Both sets of parents were kind human beings, but when it came to accepting their daughters' lesbianism, they were tentative. "Honey, are you sure? You're going to have such a hard time with this. Don't you ever want to get married and have children? We so want to be grandparents and would be such great ones." For Brenda and Alexandra, nothing anybody said mattered. They were in love; this was their life and they planned to live it to the fullest.

Over the years, both sets of parents softened. Now that they were older, they became close friends and were able to jointly embrace their daughters' lesbianism. Brenda and Alexandra were invited to all events and holidays, and both families joined in the festivities. In their mid-thirties, wanting to be parents, they adopted an infant who was readily accepted by both sets of grandparents and named Belle. Brenda's mother said, "That means beautiful from what I remember from college French. And she is."

Some years later, now a grown granddaughter, Belle, engaged to marry her college sweetheart, became a caring helper to her aging grandparents. She, her fiancé and her two mothers made sure that they were provided with what they needed, looked in on them frequently and were always available to assist. All was done willingly and with love. For this family, things went well.

GRANDPARENTS RAISING GRANDCHILDREN

You did the best you could. You and your husband had a good enough marriage, and the kids seemed okay. Your son got married. She seemed like a lovely young woman from a good family. You and her parents often had dinner together, and everything was fine. The three grandchildren went from nursery school to public school, and then the bomb exploded. "Your son and his wife were picked up for drug trafficking. They're in jail, and I don't think it will be easy for them. You'd better come downtown," said their lawyer. You unraveled. How could this be? Where did we go wrong? Is this a nightmare, or is it for real?

Their sentence was a severe one, it having been proven that they were key figures in a large drug ring. Suddenly, you and your husband, retired teachers in your mid-sixties, inherit three children, ages eight, eleven, and thirteen. As though parenting was not hard enough the first time around, you now have another unforeseen shot at it. And to make the sandwich a double-decker, one of you has an eighty-eight-year-old mother in a nursing home, whom you are used to visiting often.

Although your first instinct is to run, you know you can't and now have to juggle a zillion pieces of life at the same time. Never would you have predicted this, but you're a survivor. Somehow you'll cope. Based upon the strengths of the grandparents, this family will have a new configuration, and life will go on.

THE MULTI-GENERATIONAL AGING FAMILY

In a two-family house lived three generations: daughter, son-in-law and two sons lived on the top floor and grandma and great-grandma lived together on the main floor. Daughter worked full time, while her disabled husband was at home. Strange as it may seem, while grandma, seventy-three, had moderately severe Alzheimer's disease, great-grandma, ninety-four, was sharp as a tack and could tell you exactly what happened today, yesterday or previously, all in clear detail. She also did all the shopping and cooking and was the caregiver for the other two.

On an icy day, great-grandma fell and broke her hip on some ice. Not returning from the market at her usual time, her son-in-law was concerned. It didn't take long before the police were at the door. "Your grandma is in the hospital." Crisis befell the household. The major player had been removed, and the balance reversed in that she now had to be taken care of. Who was to be appointed caregiver? No one. The family fell apart in a drastic turn. The son-in-law had a massive coronary and died. Grandma had to be placed in a nursing home. Great-grandma had to go to a rehabilitation facility. Daughter, newly widowed and overwhelmed, had all she could do to get to work every-day and keep her job. Her two college-aged sons were away at school, and while caring, were advised to continue with their education.

This family, caring, loving and warm toward each other, was a cohesive unit. Yet, when circumstances arose where one major link was broken, the whole structure collapsed like dominoes. Great-grandma was the filling that held the sandwich together. Without her, there was no longer a sandwich.

THE LATER MARRIAGE FAMILY

I'm going for my wedding dress. It's going to be white on white with a long train, a crown on my head and a peek-a-boo veil. My friends think I'm crazy, but I'm as sane as can be. You see, I'm sixty-two years old and it's my first marriage. He's been married twice but has no children. And he's nuts about me and ten years younger. We never discuss my age.

Joy was ecstatic, but there was also concern. It came from her conversation with her eighty-seven-year-old mother. "Darling, I am so, so happy for you. Truly I had given up. You dated and dated and nothing seemed to work. And now you've found your true love. But, sweetheart, you know I've always been honest with you. You are my only child and so precious to me, but now I worry—a new husband and a new life. Will I ever see you?" Her mother tried hard to hide it, but tears rolled down her cheeks. Joy reassured her mother:

> Mom, listen, Max knows all about you. And though he's only seen you a few times, he loves you already. You are a part of me, and I am a part of you. And he said that when you come to the wedding in your wheelchair, he will wheel you down the aisle and you will be an important part of our ceremony. So, Mom, you have not lost a daughter but you have gained a son.

When family relationships are close, they run deep and stay that way. An open-faced sandwich, this one is eminently edible.

Family history cannot be rewritten. You are who you are. Your parents are who they are. Their lifetime personalities cannot be turned around, nor can their experiences with their various children, including you. But, their attitudes and perspectives and yours can be shifted somewhat, with love, understanding, and caring. Shaking a kaleidoscope opens you to new visions and experiences. Understanding your parents and yourself sets you on the path toward a good old age.

Sizing It Up

Crabbed age and youth
Cannot live together
Youth is full of pleasance
Age is full of care.

—Shakespeare

It is never easy to take on another person's burdens, even when things are going well. But there are some periods in life when it's almost inevitable. Ironically, older people may need more support just at that point when your life is the most complicated and your responsibilities are the heaviest.

You may have been living from crisis to crisis with your elders, each time hoping it is an isolated incident and that it will all go away if you don't pay attention. But it just isn't happening. Some problems have a tendency to stick and even escalate. As the idealized golden years get tarnished with the passage of time, harsh reality closes in. Now is the time to figure it out.

CHANGES

You have noticed the changes that have come with aging. Some began earlier than others. Some came on slowly and did not get out of control—others, more abruptly. Unfortunately, there is no uniform timetable. Your aunt may have shown them early, your mother or father much later, or vice versa. The differences are as varied as the individuals themselves.

The most obvious visual change brought about by aging may be the wrinkling of one's skin. But, it is important to understand that each organ system of the body changes with age at its own rate. Changes are taking place in vision, hearing, brain function, the heart, bones and on and on. For example, wrinkled eighty-year-olds, looking their age, may still retain the 20/20 vision of one fifty years younger, while experiencing declines in other areas. In addition to "normal" aging, diseases do develop, sometimes gradually and sometimes suddenly, sometimes obvious and sometimes subtle. But, change is what we can count on. What can you do? None of us has a crystal ball. The best we can do is to look at that older person and see what they're all about—who they were and still are—or are not.

LEARNING ABOUT YOUR LOVED ONE NOW

While you may have known this person for a very long time and think you know all about them, some changes may have escaped your notice. The first thing to do is to get information about your loved one's "now" condition (see table 4.1). If your relative is in a hospital with an acute (sudden-onset) illness or with an episodic worsening of a chronic disease, such as emphysema or diabetes, the treating physician is a good first source of information. If your relative is at home with chronic (ongoing) problems or an acute episode of a chronic disease, the physician may also be a good first contact. However, some elders are resistive to going to the doctor, and getting them there may be easier said than done. And others, secretive or in denial or both, don't want you to know too much.

The information you need is not all medical—it also consists of social, psychological, emotional, financial, legal and environmental factors. It's all about how your loved one is able to function now. Conditions change and so do people. What your elder needed last year or last month, or even yesterday, may not be relevant today. Observation and information gathering must be careful and continuous. What you learn will be the basis for care planning.

Table 4.1   Sizing up your relative's "now" condition

Diagnosis	What are my relative's diagnoses? Is further testing needed?
Prognosis	What is his or her chance for restoration of function/recovery?
Treatment	Options, risks, benefits and alternatives
Aftercare Needs	If hospitalized or in subacute facility, can he or she return home? If at home, what care is needed?
Other Considerations	Social, psychological, financial and legal issues

ACUTE ILLNESS

Acute illness happens. Without warning, things are changed. For Rosemary's family, depression overtook the wife and mother they knew. Things went from "just okay" to "not so bad" to "terrible" in a short period of time. When they observed the sharp decline, they had to act quickly.

Rosemary's Depression

Rosemary was a particularly beautiful woman. She always had been supersensitive and highly self-absorbed with her looks. In a long-term marriage with Tony, they had raised two daughters and a son. Their unmarried daughter, Lillian, was a teacher and chose to live at home. Tony was never more than a passive, admiring onlooker in the family system, and Lillian and her siblings usually took responsibility for family issues. Despite the fact that her mother did not like her and never hesitated to tell her, Lillian was a devoted daughter, feeling that she needed to be there for her parents and siblings.

A homemaker, Rosemary was content to maintain the household and herself. Spending much time on her appearance, she walked everyday, exercised at the gym, attended dance classes and went to the beauty salon regularly. Reading a lot about beauty and fashion, she followed it all on TV. Things rolled along. Without any forewarning, there was a drastic shift. Now in her early seventies, she became reclusive and withdrawn. "Look at me," she said. "My skin is shriveling, my eyes are not what they used to be and my breasts—well, forget it, two pancakes dried up in the pan. So, what's the use?"

When family members suggested beautifiers or plastic surgery, she looked horrified and became even more remote. Crying frequently, she would sit in a corner and stare into a mirror. Showing a sharp decline in her everyday functions, she stopped eating and drinking almost completely. No amount of talking and pleading by her family helped to change her behaviors or could convince her to seek professional help.

Eventually taken to a hospital, it was determined that there was no medical illness, and Rosemary was admitted to a psychiatric unit. There, too, she refused to eat or drink, swallow medications, or go to group therapy or activities—nor would she speak to anyone or allow anyone to speak to her. All she did, the staff reported, was sit, expressionless, and stare into the mirror for hours at a time. Asked "Mom, what do you want?" Her answer was "I want to die." Although Tony went to visit faithfully and prayed for Rosemary to get well, he deferred to his children for decision-making. And Lillian, with consultation from her siblings, took the lead.

Getting the Facts

How can you, if you were Lillian, assess this? Your first thoughts may be as follows: "How long can this go on? How much damage has been done? Why is it that she never said she wanted to die before this?" Lillian began by speaking to Rosemary's psychiatrist and other members of the hospital treatment team. What is her diagnosis? Why did it happen? Were there signs that we should have acted on sooner? What can we do now?

Treatment Options

"Your mother has a severe clinical depression with psychotic features," said the doctor. You ask, "Does she really want to die? How is she being treated? Can she actually starve herself to death? Can she be force-fed through her veins or a feeding tube? If she won't take her medications by mouth, are there shots? What other treatments are available?" The medical team explains that there are legal issues about force-feeding and medicating; however, they are also very concerned that time is running out since she is dehydrated and malnourished. They point out that medications take time to work and suggest a technique that would be quicker and more effective: electroconvulsive therapy (ECT).

Stunned, the family is instantly opposed. "ECT will make her into a vegetable. She'll never be the same again. That's what we've always heard." The team tries to calm them, explaining that ECT has been given a bad rap and that it is, in actuality, an effective treatment where time is of the essence. "Your mother will have a better chance of becoming her old self. We can't guarantee this, but we've often seen good results. We'll do the best we can." Giving the family some literature to read, they asked them to decide whether they will consent to this treatment. Still more questions follow: "What are her chances of recovery? How long must she remain in this hospital?" After a short time, Tony, the husband, as next of kin according to law, signed the consent form.

What is next for Rosemary? The family had more questions: "Could she come home some day and live with us? Would another hospital be the only resource? Or, are we looking at a nursing home? She's so young." The team expressed uncertainty as to the outcome but felt the family's decision to consent to the ECT was a positive first step. Three ECT treatments later, Rosemary asked for a comb, a mirror and a lipstick when Lillian came to visit. This gave Lillian and the family hope. The treatment team acknowledged this change but cautioned that things were still uncertain.

Faced with this uncertainty, Lillian had a lot to think about:

> How can I be true to my own self and still do what I think is right? If, on the one hand, she were to come home, that would be okay. I could deal with that. If, however, she would have to go into a facility, I would be riddled with guilt. Knowing myself, I wouldn't sleep or eat and would walk around like a zombie. I think it would kill my father, so I'd have even more

to feel guilty about. Amazingly, none of us foresaw this dramatic change. We had no idea how low things could go. What a bummer!

DEPRESSION: A PSYCHIATRIC ILLNESS

Clinical depression is more than just occasionally feeling sad or "blue." It is a serious illness that is lasting and intense and can be life-threatening. There are great variations in severity, and not all depressed individuals are like Rosemary. Presenting symptoms include physical complaints, of which the most common are insomnia, fatigue, lack of appetite, lethargy, pain and various bodily preoccupations. Observers may see emotional changes such as sadness, crying, hopelessness and a general lack of joy. Yet, when questioned, the older adult will more likely focus on the physical symptoms. In fact, depression is underreported by older persons themselves, underrecognized by informal and formal caregivers and undertreated by health professionals.

Engulfed in the dark side, the depressed person has given up. They often feel that life has nothing to offer, have no interest in activities they used to love and are convinced that no one really cares for them. And some, unfortunately, tip over into suicide. Always recognize that suicide is a potential lethal outcome of depression. Suicidal ideation may be expressed or hidden. In the case of Rosemary, she did say, every now and then, "I just want to die," as she proceeded with total neglect of herself. If a suicidal word comes up, even if it seems to be casually thrown out, take it seriously. Also, be attuned to starvation and other forms of self-neglect.

Risk factors for depression in older persons are similar to those for younger individuals, namely, being female, unmarried, widowed and under stress as well as having poor social supports. While in younger persons, the most common co-conditions are personality disorder and substance abuse, for the elderly a coexisting medical illness is the hallmark. The sleep disturbances, bodily preoccupations, loss of concentration, focus on death, anxiety and pessimism may also coincide with physical illness. For this reason, health professionals too often overlook the signs of depression or are dismissive, considering them "normative" to aging. For the sick older person, depression is a "double whammy." Additionally, depression may masquerade as or mimic a dementia or occur with it and confound the picture.

A RANGE OF DEPRESSIVE ILLNESS

Research shows that there are different kinds of depressive illness. In addition to precipitating psychological issues, usually involving loss, biological factors may also be catalysts. Certain individuals have had episodic depressions throughout their lives. For others, depression may newly occur in the older years, often associated with critical life changes such as the loss of a spouse or close others, loss of a physical ability such as vision, hearing, mobility, memory or sexual performance, loss of a career with loss of status and income, loss of a familiar dwelling or the result of alcohol or drug abuse. Depressive disorders may cause or contribute to medical illness and, conversely, medical illnesses, such as heart disease, stroke, Parkinson's disease and cancer, can cause or contribute to depression. Each condition can complicate recovery from the other.

Undeniably, the family, as a unit, will be deeply affected by the negativity, helplessness and hopelessness of the one depressed care recipient. But, you, just by your very presence, are counteracting the losses that depression is based on. And you, the caregiver, can be the one and only advocate for treatment, saving your loved one from "the emotional scrap heap" that one sufferer described.

TREATMENTS FOR DEPRESSION

It's not all bleak; depression is usually treatable. A variety of biological and psychological treatments are available. While ECT, which Rosemary received, is used in some cases, others may be treated with medications and/or some form of counseling. Combinations of these interventions have been noted to be most effective. Medications can be antidepressants or other drugs used over the short or long term, as needed, to treat specific symptoms such as sleeplessness or anxiety, or combinations. Counseling can reframe the afflicted person's negative thinking. Both long-term and short-term counseling approaches are available, and either one can be successful. The caregiver, too, may find help in learning how to deal with the depressed older adult by joining them in some sessions with the approval of the counselor. Additional help can also be derived from exercise, yoga, tai chi, acupuncture, massage, dance movement, walking, hobbies and pleasurable activities.

As in Rosemary's case, acute illness can spin your life around. It impacts the whole family. Rosemary had a psychiatric illness, but in older people medical illness is even more common.

STROKE: A LEADING CAUSE OF DISABILITY

Stroke happens when a part of the brain loses its blood supply. Some strokes kill, some leave significant disabilities, and some are unknown to the victim. The severity depends upon what part of the brain was affected and how much tissue was destroyed. The majority of people survive strokes and regain some or all of their capacities. Many require extensive rehabilitation and caregiving services. While there has been more attention paid to the prevention of stroke by controlling risk factors such as high blood pressure and heart abnormalities, stroke remains a frequent cause of death and disability.

Matthew: Victim of a Disabling Stroke

Matthew, a seventy-two-year-old attorney, felt dizzy after returning from lunch. "What was it that I ate? The shrimp seemed okay, and the iced tea was good. So why this funny feeling now; my head seems as if it's not mine." Then he felt some tingling in his right arm. By the time he called his secretary, he was unsteady and had trouble getting the words out. She called the paramedics. When they arrived, they recognized it for what it was: a stroke. Rushed to the hospital, his right side became paralyzed and his speech affected. For the first forty-eight hours, the prognosis was uncertain. Matthew's vibrant sixty-eight-year-old wife, Helen, was called and rushed to his bedside. Since there were no children, she alerted his younger brother and law partner, Bob.

Helen and Bob were brimming over with questions: "How did the stroke happen to an active, seemingly healthy man? Were there signs we should have seen? What are his chances of a complete recovery? What are his needs for aftercare?" The physician answered the questions one by one.

After a stay of one week, the treatment team suggested that Matthew be transferred to a rehabilitation facility for physical therapy, speech therapy, occupational therapy, cognitive therapy and nursing care. It was explained that rehabilitation is provided in a specialized rehabilitation facility, a subacute facility, a subacute unit in a nursing home (skilled nursing facility), a "swing bed" in an acute hospital or at home. The physician suggested that Matthew needed transitional care in a specialized facility before he would be ready to return home, which was Helen's and Matthew's preference. The discharge planner gave Helen a list of facilities.

What to Look for in a Rehabilitation Facility

Helen was bewildered and did not know what to make of the "choices" that were suggested to her. Helen could ask Matthew's physician, check things out on the web and ask friends. Once she has narrowed the list to a few facilities, Helen should make personal visits to see how they strike her. There are several criteria to consider, including availability of needed services, accessibility of the facility and quality (see table 4.2).

Table 4.2   Criteria for selecting a nursing home for rehabilitation and long-term care

Phone calls/websites/maps

1. Availability of needed services—occupational therapy, physical therapy, speech therapy, cognitive therapy—different facilities may differ in frequency and intensity. Do they perform intravenous infusion on site, if your patient requires this?
2. Medicare/Medicaid certification or contract with your insurance company, if patient has "managed care plan." These will determine sources of payment that could be available to you in addition to out-of-pocket payments.
3. Accessibility for caregiver—the nearer to home the better.
4. Quality—per Nursing Home Inspection Report (www.nursinghomecompare.com), Department of Health query or reports by friends and family.
5. Allied (transfer) hospitals, should loved one require rehospitalization.
6. List of physicians who see patients in the facility.

Personal visit/observation

1. Ambience/comfort level visiting/cleanliness/grooming of patients.
2. Staffing—how many caregiving staff to each patient on each shift? The number is an indicator; however, attentiveness and prompt response to requests and call bells is an even more important indicator.
3. Attitude and demeanor of staff. Observe: Are they friendly and polite? Are they receptive to answering your questions?
4. Activities—is there a variety of activities that your patient can enjoy?
5. Quality—review their latest inspection report.
6. Family visitors—do they seem content? Ask them while you're visiting.

Frantic and scared at the thought of needing to send her husband to a nursing home even temporarily, Helen accepted Bob's offer to go along for moral support. What should she look for? Cleanliness of the facility, the appearance of the patients, staff-to-patient ratio, the responsiveness and availability of staff to patients, hours of rehabilitation actually provided each day and the receptivity of staff to her visit and her questions. She should feel welcome and be treated with dignity. What is the allied hospital, should Matthew require a sudden rehospitalization? And last but far from least, who picks up the tab?

Paying for In-Patient Rehabilitation

While Medicare is the major payment source, there are copayments that may be charged to the family, depending on whether there is other insurance and what kind. Helen must find out whether the facility is certified by Medicare (most are). The facility will provide an estimate of the out-of-pocket charges and the anticipated length of stay. The Medicare benefit is determined by the condition and progress of the patient. If it runs out, the patient will have to pay privately for any time beyond the limit or may have to seek Medicaid or other benefits for long-term care.

What was next for Matthew? What will happen when Matthew is discharged to return to his home? How much will he be able to do for himself? Will he be able to be left alone safely—for two hours, for four hours or not at all? Helen, at sixty-eight, is now the primary caregiver. An avid golfer and club member, where do her energies go? Although changed, Helen has a life, too. While she may need to curtail some of her activities, hiring a home health aide would enable her to find a balance and do both. This could be full time or part time. In any event, Helen and the aide will need to observe Matthew for any new symptoms or problems and follow up with his doctor.

Matthew is now a disabled person, and his home environment must be adapted to his changed needs. For example, if there is an upstairs bedroom, he may need to move downstairs. What about the bathroom—is the doorway wide enough for a wheelchair? Can he reach the sink? Can he get into the shower, and is it safe? If not, changes have to come about. Prior to discharge, staff from the rehabilitation facility should be asked to visit the home and make recommendations. In the bathroom, they may suggest adding items such as grab bars in the shower and around the toilet, a shower chair, a handheld shower and a raised toilet seat. If the facility does not provide this service, they may refer Helen to a local home health-care program. While there will be a fee for this service, it is worth it as safety is always a primary concern.

What about the future? Losing any part of speech is catastrophic for an attorney, and may force Matthew to retire. How would retirement change their lifestyle? Can Helen feel comfortable taking a larger role in financial management? If not, she needs to seek advice. This may be available from their lawyer, accountant or financial planner.

Both Helen and Matthew had their lives turned upside down. Thrust into new roles as decision maker and caregiver, Helen would have to seek advice to master this. A loving, devoted wife, she would move into a whole new world. How would she face it? But face it she would. And she did.

Strokes vary in severity and intensity, and the outcomes can be different. Service requirements vary, and not everyone has to make the same decisions. Carmen's daughter, Olivia, did not. In Carmen's case, the stroke turned out to be mild enough that, with a thoughtful lifestyle change, she was able to find new friends and new interests.

Carmen: Surviving a Milder Stroke

Carmen, a thin, agile seventy-year-old, who worked as a teacher's aide, came home from school one afternoon and felt "strange" enough to call her daughter, Olivia, and ask her to come over. When Olivia arrived, she noticed that her mother's speech was slurred. Suspecting a stroke, she called 9-1-1. It was a stroke. Although fairly mild, Carmen was hospitalized.

A widow, Carmen lived alone in a modest home in an urban area that was experiencing a downturn. She drove her old car, which was still in good condition. She owned a small house free and clear. Her job provided extra income and health-care benefits that included excellent prescription drug coverage. Fiercely independent, she was active in her church. She enjoyed close relationships with Olivia, her only child, and her ten-year-old grand-daughter, Evangelica.

When she was discharged after several days, her motor skills were intact; however, her speech was scrambled. She could not get the words out. And when she tried, it was like word salad. Her recent memory was also mildly affected. A Magnetic Resonance Imaging (MRI) of the brain revealed that there had been two previously unknown ministrokes. Olivia was concerned that Carmen's physician had allowed her high blood pressure to remain poorly controlled and was now determined to help her mother find better medical care.

What was next for Carmen? At discharge, Carmen agreed to stay at Olivia's home while receiving speech therapy. She wanted to return home alone; however, the professionals they consulted determined that Carmen would not be safe alone at home if she could not use the telephone to make her needs known. Speech therapy yielded only a partial recovery. It was suggested that assisted living in a nearby community would be a viable alternative, enabling family and friends to visit and Carmen to continue her church involvements. She would also be in a safer neighborhood and not burdened by her house and car.

With her available funds and the sale of the house, there were enough resources for several years of care. Olivia prescouted facilities and found one that she felt would be most comfortable for her mom. Then, Olivia, Carmen and Evangelica went to check it out. Everyone liked it.

Upon moving into the Assisted Living Facility, Carmen saw a former coworker, renewed the friendship and made a remarkable adjustment. She lives in a large studio apartment with her own furniture and mementoes, eats three meals a day in a beautiful dining room, has her apartment cleaned and maintained, participates in a full calendar of activities and is driven to church and doctors' appointments. Her medications are administered, and a nurse monitors her health. Family and friends visit often. Says Carmen, "What could be bad?"

While Carmen was able to adapt to her new circumstances, Olivia was apprehensive about breaking up her mother's home. It wasn't easy to make that decision to place her mother in assisted living, no matter how attractive. Feeling guilt that her own home did not have an extra bedroom, she recognized that Carmen would be isolated and alone all day, since she, Olivia, worked full time. Despite her anxiety, she accomplished the change with sensitivity and compassion and visited her mother frequently. Her experience was positive and uplifting. "Whoever said aging is all downhill should come and visit my mother," she volunteered.

CHRONIC MEDICAL ILLNESS WITH ACUTE PROBLEMS

Ella's later years would certainly appear to others as "downhill," but don't tell her that. She wanted more than anything else to be cared for at home with her family. Her values, beliefs and preferences were so strong that, once she got over the trauma of her amputation, they propelled her through the rehabilitation process, her ticket to get back home. That was the only place she wanted to be.

Ella: A Believer in Family Care

Seventy-year-old Ella, a long-standing diabetic, lives in a single family home with her extended family. She has two single daughters and two grandsons. Widowed for many years, Ella, the matriarch, rules the roost. In addition to her diabetes, she has kidney disease requiring dialysis three times a week and infected leg wounds that led to an amputation on one side. A protracted hospitalization was followed by an extended stay in a rehabilitation facility. At the time of her discharge home, Ella's situation was medically complex, and there were multiple factors to assess and plan for.

The home was an older one, with little handicapped accessibility. Basic changes were made: a ramp was built from the garage into the house and the door widened to make it accessible for her wheelchair; her bedroom door was widened for the wheelchair, the furniture rearranged and her closet modified so that she could access it independently; the bathroom was enlarged by annexing space from an adjoining room, and a "drive-in" shower with a seat and grab bars was constructed. The kitchen table was also replaced, so that she could wheel right up and, as is her style, be a part of family mealtimes.

Because of her multiple complications, she required close monitoring and supervision and frequent medical visits, which the daughters pitched in to do. Though willing caregivers, they realized they could not do it alone and made the following arrangements: A home health aide was hired to assist with personal care on a daily basis. Dialysis at a nearby facility, with transport by ambulette, was arranged for three times a week. A home health agency was enlisted to provide nursing services for her wounds, physical therapy, occupational therapy and nutritional counseling. Home delivery of wound care supplies, diabetes testing items, incontinence products and medications was arranged.

Ella's care is complex and expensive. Fortunately, she is entitled to health-care benefits from both Medicare and Medicaid. At home, Medicare will pay for her wound care and other skilled nursing, therapies, some supplies and dialysis; Medicaid will pay for the home health aide, the medical transportation and supplies.

Very importantly, there is a smooth-running, supportive and willing family, with members who work as a team, sharing the same beliefs, values and understandings of life. Hard working, they never begrudged their caregiving responsibilities, which they performed with grace and cheerfulness. Needless to say, Ella was grateful to be home again and "there" for her beloved grandchildren.

LONG-TERM PROGRESSIVE ILLNESS

In some situations, there is the opportunity to plan early on, so that wishes and resources can be accommodated. And things can be adjusted as needs change over the long haul. This is what happened with Dorothy.

Dorothy: When Dementia Was Added to the Menu

Dorothy, a widow of sixty-eight, works in a café she owns with her son, Sean, and daughter-in-law, Carol. Her other son, Tim, is career military and lives overseas with his family. Communication is by phone and e-mail, and they get together once a year. Dorothy, Sean and Carol work hard to keep up with the latest food preferences and styles—low carb, low fat and lower calorie—and they have a faithful clientele. Dorothy does the food ordering and works as the cashier, while Sean and Carol manage the kitchen and the staff. One day, Sean and Carol began noticing some changes in Dorothy's grooming, nothing big but little food stains, wrinkled blouses, missing buttons on a favorite dress and mismatched jewelry. They attributed this to Dorothy's recent bout with the flu with a high fever.

Then, Dorothy started to repeat herself. She became impatient, argumentative and even confrontational at times, very different from her usual personality style. Her children shrugged it off, saying, "No big deal. She's remarkable for her age." Not too many months later, she seemed a little confused—couldn't always make change—and things began not to add up. Her memory seemed to be slipping.

Concerned that something bad was happening to Dorothy, Carol begged Sean to talk with his mother and insist that she go for a medical checkup. Dorothy saw her doctor and reported that "everything checked out." When things did not improve, Carol did some research, found a Center on Aging at a hospital in a nearby city and made an appointment for Dorothy to have a comprehensive Geriatric Assessment, reassuring Dorothy that she would go with her.

The Geriatric Assessment: What Is It?

A Geriatric Assessment is a comprehensive evaluation of an older person, performed by a team of specialists trained in the field of aging and the special problems of elders. Members of this team usually include physicians specializing in geriatric medicine, neurology and psychiatry, nurses, social workers and psychologists. The team is particularly attuned to problems such as memory loss, falling, incontinence, use of multiple medications and the interactions among different medical conditions. Be aware that, much as it is needed, not every facility has a geriatric specialization.

Dorothy consulted the team due to her memory loss. Over three appointments, she had a complete physical examination, laboratory studies, imaging of her brain (an MRI), a consultation with a neurologist and neuropsychological testing. Results were presented at a conference where Dorothy was present. The findings were that "Dorothy has Alzheimer's disease, mild now, but likely to worsen over time." Medications were prescribed that could possibly slow the progress of the disease but would not stop or reverse it. The team indicated to Dorothy that she was fortunate to get an early diagnosis and strongly suggested that she and her family actively plan for the future. "Fortunate or a disaster," thought Dorothy.

The team would see Dorothy every three months, or more often if necessary, to monitor her health. They provided a list of resources, including the Alzheimer's Association, professional geriatric care managers and eldercare attorneys. Dorothy's was a complex situation—social, emotional, financial (she co-owned the business and the two-family house where they all lived) and legal (she had never had a Power of Attorney drawn up or any written indication of her wishes for health care). The team recommended that the family engage a professional geriatric care manager to help them sort through the maze of issues, coordinate their planning efforts and provide emotional support. The family was devastated. They never thought they'd hear the "A word" applied to them. Carol started to be hit with fears and anxiety: "Will Sean end up this way, too? And how will this affect our kids?"

Planning for the Long Haul

Dorothy and her family were caught in a storm and had to protect themselves from the lightning that was sure to strike. Alzheimer's is a disease that progresses downward, but at different rates in different people. Understanding this is critical, and planning must accommodate changes in her condition over time.

The family consulted a geriatric care manager to help them develop a plan and also hired an attorney to work with their legal affairs. Knowing that Dorothy loved to work, they would encourage her to continue and be carefully observant and sensitive to her failings. Since they lived in a two-family house, they could also be closely attentive, responding to any situation needing immediate intervention. They would take one step at a time.

Stella and George: When Life Has Its Own Design

In their mid-seventies, Stella and George were healthy, active and in a long-standing, loving marriage. They had two sons, John and Terry. John, a forty-eight-year-old sales manager, who loved sunshine and water sports, moved from New York City to Florida a few years ago with his wife, Tina, and their family. His parents chose to remain up north, with his mother, a wink in her eye, saying, "And you know, Johnny, Florida has too many old people." The second son, Terry, remained in New York City, with his wife, Ilene.

One morning at 5:00 A.M., there was a sharp ring. Trying hard not to wake Tina, John grabbed at the phone. "Yes?" he asked. He could barely hear the muffled voice at the other end. "Speak a little louder, please. I can't hear you, and it's only five a.m., you know." "Sorry." It was his younger brother. "Terry," John whispered, "What's the matter? Are you okay?" Then came the barely recognizable words. "John," whispered Terry, "Dad died."

John burst out, "Oh, my God. That can't be. I just spoke to him yesterday. He seemed fine." Terry said,

> I know, but later in the night, he had some chest pains. Mom thought it was because he overate. But they didn't go away. Instead, they became stronger and stronger. Mom was hysterical. She called me. I called 9-1-1. Putting a coat over my pajamas, I ran over. By the time I got there, Pop was in the ambulance, and Mom and I went with him to the hospital.
>
> The police, the paramedics and the doctors were all wonderful. We hoped for a miracle, but it was not to be. Dad died just after he arrived. As quickly as you flick a match and blow it out, his soul had left his body.

John was silent, until he heard himself saying, "So, Mom is now a widow."

WIDOWHOOD

Plunged into widowhood, Stella is now feeling her way into a new world, one that is unknown, unfamiliar and full of darkness and uncertainty. She now has to learn how to survive. It's not that she was just dependent on George but rather that she had somebody in her life that she loved. Now a piece of her was gone.

The loss of a partner is a devastating occurrence, followed by a period of grief and disruption. Mourning usually involves a number of emotional reactions: numbness, apathy, longing, sorrow, remorse and guilt, as well as physical symptoms including insomnia and fatigue. There are differences, of course, depending on the individual and the intensity and closeness of the relationship. The duration of the emotional and physical reactions also varies.

For the sons, who are also grieving, the loss is theirs as well. Yet, they must carry on. They may want to rush in with some particular solution such as, "Mom, come live with one of us." However, the new widow may need her own time and space before she is ready to make important decisions. For Stella, it is her choice as to how she wants to live. She may want to stay exactly where she is or make a change such as taking in a boarder or moving to a different home.

Stella is at a precipice and needs time. This is not the time for planning. What Terry and John can do is be sensitive to her feelings, listen empathically, show genuine concern and let their mother know that they are there for her.

All born different, we age differently. Over time, change comes in a variety of shapes, sizes, and at different rates. Sneaking up on you gradually or suddenly seeming to knock you over, it does not necessarily proceed in a straight line. There are ups and downs. There is no single scenario, no "one size fits all" solution. Knowing the care recipient and their needs and responses is paramount. And knowing yourself completes the picture. Understanding this is critical to how to stay sane and survive.

· 5 ·

Planning:
Developing a Blueprint

$\mathcal{O}$nce you've sized up your loved one's situation and developed a snapshot, you now face the challenge of developing a more comprehensive portrait, with all its beauty and all of its blemishes. You have identified the problems and addressed them for the short term. Now, it is time to develop a blueprint for the longer-term plan. Like a budget, this plan is an approximation, a guide. The point is to cut down on future crises by anticipating, rather than reacting to, the issues.

ESTABLISHING A DIALOGUE

A good first step is to start a dialogue. Ideally, when you start planning for the future, things will not have reached a boiling point, and you will be able to have a discussion with your elder about their situation. If receptive and able to participate, your work is cut out for you. Sometimes, there is no rush; at other times, the period for planning becomes truncated by necessity, as in the case of an acute illness or a drastic change in the caregiver's situation.

CONVENING A FAMILY CONFERENCE

The goal of the conference is to examine problems and reach for solutions. If your loved one cannot participate, you may convene a family conference without them. Logistical, medical, legal, psychological and financial factors are important, as is the identification of professionals needed to assist you.

Holding this conference may be a challenge. Not all families run smoothly. Old conflicts may surface and make for bumps in the road. Brothers Zach and Claude carry their rivalry to the present day.

53

Zach and Claude: The Rivals

"You're the favorite one—and always took advantage. Mom and Pop never saw it, but I saw through you. And now that they're older, you do nothing for them. Always some excuse: busy, busy, busy. So who does it all? Me."

Zach is three years younger than Claude and is now a doctor. Claude is an attorney. The parents always referred to Zach as "our son, the doctor," but ignored Claude and the good work he did as a noted prosecuting attorney.

Now, some decisions had to be made. Their parents were in their eighties, their father becoming so disoriented that sometimes he went out in his pajamas on a cold night. The neighbors were horrified. Their mother could no longer see too well and had no idea of what her husband was doing. Something had to be done immediately. The two brothers could not agree. Claude said, "If we don't do something now, I can't predict what will happen, but it won't be great." But Zach answered, "You're such a worrier. Slow down. They're okay. I have to run now." A family conference was not to be.

THE CONFERENCE

When a conference does take place, who should attend? Generally, the first meeting should be without the care recipient; however, this is situation specific. In some cases, the care recipient may call the meeting. It would be best if all the siblings could be present; however, if distance or logistics prevents this, perhaps they can be there via a conference call. Spouses or significant others can be briefed by their mates afterward. It is highly desirable to have a moderator—a social worker, discharge planner, physician, counselor, geriatric care manager, clergyperson—someone who knows the case and can make sure that there is an opportunity for everyone to speak. The moderator will also help to keep things moving along, on track and on schedule.

Where should the meeting be? It should be held in a family member's home, if this will be comfortable for all, or at a neutral spot, such as the moderator's office or a hospital or nursing home conference room.

When should the meeting be scheduled? Plan it for as soon as possible after the occurrence or recognition of the problem and at a time that would be convenient for most attending. More than one meeting may be needed.

The Setup

How should things be set up? It is best to have as much information as possible available, including applicable documents, such as Durable Power of Attorney, Health-Care Proxy, Living Will and health, long-term care and life insurance policies. A copy of the birth certificate and the Social Security card will also be needed. And make an inventory of whatever else is there.

A formal agenda should be developed by the moderator with input from the siblings. But, don't get hung up over the form. It is the substance that counts. You need to start communicating. One person should be designated to take notes, which will be the basis for further action. Remember, all in attendance need a chance to speak, even if their opinion is not popular. A sample agenda is contained in table 5.1.

Table 5.1   Agenda for family conference(s)

Facts:
Diagnosis (or diagnoses)
☐   Need for further evaluation
☐   Desire for another medical opinion(s)
☐   Treatment options, including risks, benefits, alternatives and costs
Prognosis
☐   Course
☐   Potential outcome
☐   Time frame
☐   Possible complications/recurrences
Medical Treatment
☐   Options: immediate and future
☐   Care recipient wishes
☐   Venue
☐   Participation in research

Immediate Concerns:
☐   Documents establishing wishes
☐   Decision-making ability of care recipient
    —   Availability of finances for care
    —   Resistance to care by care recipient
☐   Identifying the primary caregiver
☐   Overall management
    —   Division of labor among family members
    —   Resolving disputes

Logistics:
☐   Housing
    —   Immediate and for the future
☐   Transportation

Legal Issues:
☐   Now and for the future
    —   Business ownership, home ownership, vested authority

Finances:
☐   Now
☐   Access
☐   Available insurance
☐   Current and potential entitlements

What Should Be Discussed?

Their current health should be discussed: review the facts, establishing what the diagnosis (condition) is, what the course of the illness will likely be and the expected outcome (prognosis). At this point, consider whether further evaluation, other medical opinions, or treatment at a different facility are necessary. Also, know the treatment options, including the benefits, risks, costs, alternatives and logistics for each.

Your father has just been diagnosed with a rare but virulent cancer. You have been told about the available treatment options, their risks, benefits and alternatives. The odds are not in his favor. You have heard about some more aggressive treatment protocols in another area of the country, and your sister has heard about a treatment available only overseas. Your father is overwrought, highly anxious and unwilling to talk about his case. Previously, he said, "I wouldn't want to be tortured when I'm going to die anyway." But that was in the abstract, and he never wrote anything down. There is no Living Will, nor is there a designated Health-Care Proxy. And now that there is a real issue, an urgent condition, he's unwilling to discuss it. While you remember his statement, he never repeated it. Did he really mean it?

Do you opt for minimum treatment or more? Would the more aggressive treatments be commensurate with his wishes? Are you ready to drop everything and go great distances on a gamble? What will be the costs of such a venture? What if there are complications that occur when he's back at home? Would his local doctor be willing to work with you? If not, who will? These are your choices. If you are considering a geographically distant treatment, you may have to think about relocating for the time being. This way you will be close to the treating physician. Otherwise, discuss the plan with your father's doctor and seek his or her collaboration.

Their Mental State

Consider the mental state of the care recipient. Do you think that they are able to make decisions regarding their own affairs and care? Is their mental state likely to improve? Are there documents appointing a substitute decision maker (proxy) or expressing wishes for health care (directive)? If not, who among the siblings has had any discussions with the parent about their wishes? Would your parent want to be a part of a research program? And, if so, under what conditions? How is their emotional state? Are they depressed, in denial, hypochondriacal or resistant to care?

Their Strengths and Weaknesses

Do they need supervision or personal care? Are they able to remain in or return to their own home? Can they direct or supervise their own help? Are home modifications needed? What beliefs and preferences have they expressed? Don't forget to pay attention to their strengths.

Their Financial Status

What is the financial situation of the care recipient? Have you or one of your siblings looked around the house and in every corner and under every pile for checkbooks, bank statements, brokerage account statements, bonds and cash? Have you located insurance policies and benefit statements? Have you found insurance cards, such as Medicare, Medigap or Medicaid? Obviously, everything you have found belongs to them. Make an inventory. Based on what you have found, are there funds available for treatment and management now? Their financial resources will affect care planning for both now and the future.

RESOLVING DISPUTES

A mechanism for resolution of disputes is necessary. Conflicts may arise around different issues: the nature of care (standard care versus experimental); aggressive intervention versus palliative (comfort) care; the site of care (one hospital versus another, in-home versus a long-term care facility); and the professional consultants on whom you choose to rely. If there is a single designated Health-Care Proxy, they may act according to the authority given them in the existing document and may consider or overrule objections voiced by their siblings. Where all are empowered equally, there is a need to come to an agreement regarding how disputes are to be settled—perhaps majority rules or resolution with the assistance of a designated outside person. If there are disputes over finances, then the Power of Attorney has the final word.

THE ONLY CHILD

You are an only child. What should you do? Have a meeting with a professional and bring your spouse or a good friend along. Maybe you will also want to bring a cousin, niece or aunt, who is actively involved in the family system and may be a potential caregiving teammate. Remember, the caregiving may already be or become a big job that you cannot do alone. You will need all the help you can get—from family, friends, neighbors and professionals.

Mary Lou: The Only Child

Mary Lou has young children and a demanding job and lives across the country from her elderly mother, Flora. Widowed and with little social support, Flora's finances are limited. Mary Lou received a message from a discharge planner that Flora "was hospitalized suddenly, can no longer live alone and needs a placement." Surprised, Mary Lou called her mother and found her confused, with no ability to provide any information other than "I'm sick." Mary Lou repeatedly tried to contact the discharge planner and got only voice mail. She was not able to drop everything and get on a plane, since her husband was away on a business trip, nor could she sit by the phone indefinitely and wait for a return call. Stymied, she decided to hire a geriatric care manager in her mother's locale. She called the National Association of Professional Geriatric Care Managers (520-881-8008 or www.caremanager.org).

The care manager visited Flora, did an assessment and spoke with hospital staff. Agreeing that Flora could no longer live alone, she discussed the options with Mary Lou. Having found an appropriate facility, she implemented the placement. Mary Lou said the care manager "saved me a lot of worry, and I now know that my mother is being taken care of." Planning to visit in the very near future, Mary Lou will close her mother's apartment at that time.

Setting up a family conference may be ideal, but the procedure must be tailored to the situation. While cases may have common threads, every case is different. For Mary Lou, the only child, the "who" for the meeting was obvious, the "when" was immediately and the "where" became the telephone and e-mail. The agenda was clear. The need for action was urgent. Thousands of miles away from her mother, she could not get the facts and had to take whatever shortcuts she could.

THE PRIMARY CAREGIVER

Someone needs to be in charge. Who will be the primary caregiver? Sometimes, it is obvious, where one child has been taking the lead and is willing and able to continue in this role. There is agreement among the siblings that this is the best arrangement, and they will be supportive of each other. In other families, there may be no trust among the siblings, and old rivalries and conflicts often resurface. Underlying dissension may be a competition to be the "best child" or a desire to look after an inheritance they believe is an entitlement. Situations and motivations vary. Compromise is needed at the outset.

Should you be the primary caregiver? Now is the time to begin to size things up and consider what would be best. Questions push at you. What has my loved one been like? What are they like now? What do they need? What do they want? How do I, with my limited knowledge about aging, decide on the right course of action? Can I be the primary caregiver? What are my strengths? What are my limitations? How much energy can I realistically expend? And how do I handle the family "hot spots"? How do we get out of the swampland and into the sunlight? And, most of all, where do I start?

DEFINING RESPONSIBILITIES

Identify the immediate needs of the care recipient. Establish goals. Set up a detailed plan of actions needed to achieve these goals. Appoint a family member for responsibilities such as home maintenance, patient care supervision, escort to medical appointments, bill paying and liaison with physicians, insurance and lawyers. The responsibilities depend on the strengths and weaknesses of the doers and vary in frequency and intensity, according to the situation, but mutual support is always preferred.

Define the Duties

One daughter will be responsible for the day-to-day activities, such as hiring, managing and supervising the home-care workers, preparing the medications and communicating with the physicians. The other will do the grocery shopping and home maintenance. Both will escort mom to medical appointments. The third sibling, who is geographically remote, but the designated Power of Attorney, will manage the finances, pay the bills and deal with the insurance companies and lawyers. A fourth sibling wants to give advice but will not agree to take any responsibility. What to do? You can let them vent. Despite feeling angry, you can simply let it go. Or, maybe over time, the sibling will reconsider and decide that playing ball is the better way to go.

Create a Daily Routine

It is always necessary to have an overall plan. For the person requiring at-home care, it is key to establish a detailed schedule. Credence should always be given to the wishes and preferences of the elder. They are who they are and became who they are over a period of years. For an elder who has always slept until later in the morning, do not start the day at seven o'clock. Conversely, if Dad always got up at six o'clock, make sure that this is taken into account.

The day usually begins with personal care—bathing, dressing and grooming. Who will do this, when and how often? It is desirable to normalize the care recipient's appearance as much as possible. For example, the woman who is accustomed to having her hair colored and styled by a beautician should have this service on a regular basis. The man who wore a tie every day to work is used to this and should continue even though his situation has changed.

And there is no excuse for dirty, stained or torn clothing. Compliments about appearance are always in order—"what a pretty dress, nice lipstick, great tie!" Self-esteem can never be overvalued.

Toileting is an issue for those who need help with it. The care recipient may need to be taken to the toilet on a regular schedule, perhaps every two hours, or reminded or cued to go. In addition, the elder may require assistance with personal hygiene. If incontinent and requiring a diaper, regular changes and meticulous skin care are essential to avoid discomfort and skin breakdown.

Manage Medications

Even for the most capable, management of multiple medications can be daunting. But, for the frail elder, forgetfulness, limited vision, poor coordination or unclear instructions can lead to dangerous errors. In fact, medication interactions or errors are the most common reason for elders' trips to Emergency Rooms. How do you get around this? Someone, who is available most of the time and knows the situation, needs to take responsibility. For the person who lives alone and has no family nearby, this can be a willing neighbor or friend. Medications must be set up in an organized way. Dosage schedules require simplification with a goal of as much consistency as possible—before, with or after meals. Work with the physician and pharmacist to establish the best schedule. Medications that are no longer needed should be thrown out.

Arrange Meals and Activities

Meals should be as pleasant and joyful as possible. Good nutrition is always essential. The family and home health aide must know the care recipient's preferences and limitations, such as allergies, difficulty swallowing, problems using utensils, or an inability to feed themselves. Sometimes, individuals who receive some personal care at home may be able to go to a senior center or an adult day program for lunch and socialization. The schedule of other activities and appointments needs to be known and managed. Not to be underestimated is the need for transportation to enable them to get to their activities.

FALL PREVENTION

Falls are all too common among the elderly and can result in diminished quality of life or even death. Active prevention is an absolute must. Hazards, such as loose throw rugs and other obstacles, must be removed. Furniture should be sturdy and in good repair. Chairs with arms are helpful. Slippery floors are to be avoided. Glare-proof and even lighting is desirable. For added support, railings should be available on both sides of stairways. Bathrooms should be adapted for safety, for instance, raised toilet seat and grab bars, grab bars and seat in shower and skid-proof matting underfoot. Mobility aids such as canes, walkers and wheelchairs need to be easily accessible and in good repair. The patient, family and health-care aide must be instructed in their use and maintenance. Clutter must be removed. Clear walking paths need to be maintained in the home, so that the person can move about freely and safely.

Chris: The Frail Elder with His Own Plan

An eighty-year-old widower, Chris lives in senior housing in the small midwestern town where he raised his children and cared for his wife until her death. His family is emotionally close, although geographically somewhat distant. He has two married sons and six grandchildren. Paul, his oldest son, lives sixty miles away in a city, and his other son, Eric, is a plane ride away in another city. The grandchildren are scattered. Both daughters-in-law work full time. Chris had a serious stroke to which he almost succumbed. He was airlifted to a major medical center in Paul's home city for neurosurgery. After a bumpy course, he recovered enough to be sent to a rehabilitation facility. Insisting on going to a facility in his home town, Chris would have no part of a place near either son, no matter how much they tried to convince him of the benefits.

Rehabilitation went well. Left with a weak leg, a limp and some word-finding and mild memory problems, he was sent home with a walker and a prescription for outpatient rehabilitation, although not permitted to drive.

His sons pleaded with him to come to live with or near one of them, but Chris adamantly refused. He wanted to remain in his own home and go back to the same facility for outpatient rehabilitation. His plan was to use the town's senior transport to get to rehab and the doctor, his neighbor and part-time housekeeper would increase her hours a little, and he'd get Meals on Wheels for lunch or eat at the rehab center. Worried that his care arrangements were rather weak, especially since he was alone at night, his family held their breath.

Although he would not accept as much care as the family believed he needed, Chris agreed to turn over managing his finances and paying his bills to his son, Paul, giving him Power of Attorney, and named his other son, Eric, a Health-Care Proxy, neither of which had been in place at the time of his stroke. At least they had begun a dialog for the future.

Chris's plan lasted for about six months. Not driving was a much bigger deterrent to his lifestyle than he had imagined. He found that he couldn't fill the big gaps of time when he constantly had to be asking others for rides.

Much as he had refused his sons' and daughters-in law's suggestions at the time of hospital discharge, he obviously had heard it all. One day, he called his son, Paul, and asked him if he would take him to "that assisted living near him." Surprised, Paul did.

Almost instantly, Chris said he liked it and arranged to move in. Although it was different from his prior living arrangement, high-rise versus a garden apartment, urban versus small town, he adjusted quickly and enjoyed the activities and the added benefit of being near enough to his son and daughter-in-law that he could go over to their home for dinner and eat with the family. With the move, his walking improved as did his word finding. So far, so good. And, last we heard, Chris has developed "eyes for the woman across the hall."

DOES THE HOME FIT THE "NOW" CONDITION?

Should elder parents remain in their residence? Does it match their current condition? Look around and ask yourself some questions. Are there architectural features that are no longer suitable? Is it high on a hill that leaves them short of breath when they're out even for a short walk? Is there a bathroom on every level, or must they climb stairs when they are not steady on their feet? Is it expensive to maintain? Is it drafty and costly to heat, even though they use only a small portion of it? Is the landscaping expensive to maintain? Is the rent or real estate tax out of proportion to their current income? Are they insisting on remaining in their home only to conserve it as a "legacy for the children?"

What about social supports? Are they isolated from family, friends and neighbors or remote from public transportation? Have their friends and acquaintances moved from the neighborhood? Are they unable to access help in an emergency? Are they really struggling, despite their protestations? If you've answered "yes" to several of these questions, it is time to think about making a change.

EMERGENCY RESPONSE SYSTEMS

An in-between step may be to get a personal emergency response system, usually a pendant hooked into the telephone system that can be pressed to reach a central station monitor in the case of an emergency. This is for people who are at risk of falling, have medical conditions that may require emergency help or just opt for peace of mind. These are usually available for a fairly reasonable monthly fee. Medicaid may cover this for its beneficiaries. Assisted living facilities may also provide these helpful aids.

Individuals living alone find this apparatus reassuring, knowing they can obtain assistance when they need it. Agnes, who had severely arthritic and painful knees and hips, which made her prone to falling, found this helpful. "It makes me feel so protected." On the other hand, simple as these devices are to use, an individual with dementia may not be able to figure them out—or remember to use it when the critical time comes. Well partners of individuals with dementia find these devices helpful, since they can use them to summon help when they can no longer rely on their impaired mate.

LOOKING AT HOUSING OPTIONS

While homes can be renovated to better meet the needs of their occupants, there are other issues to consider, including expenses and saddling the family with too many chores. And despite the loneliness and isolation experienced by the elder, location is not always changeable.

What about having your parent move in with you, using a bedroom of one of your grown kids or adding a room and modifying or adding a bathroom? What would this involve? How would this affect your privacy and lifestyle? Would your spouse be able to handle the disruption? Would they be able to "share" you with your parent? How much pressure would caregiving put on you, even if you hired help?

At home care is not always easy. Requiring planning, supervision and coordination, it can be labor intensive and time consuming. And, depending on what is needed, home care may be expensive.

Everyone is unique, and there is no "one size fits all" plan. Creative approaches can be developed. Judy, her daughter and her son in law worked one out.

Judy

Judy, a new Medicare recipient, who has had rheumatoid arthritis for many years, continues to work as a professional at a mental health clinic not far from home. Despite her physical limitations and pain, she manages to continue working. Driving an adapted car and walking with a walker, she attends cultural events when she is able.

Living alone in a large home, she has a young boarder, a college student who, in exchange for a low rent, helps with household chores and errands but has only limited time. Her married daughter, Lana, Lana's husband, Evan, and their three young children live a four-hour car ride away. While their contact is usually by phone with visits on holidays, their emotional ties have always been close.

Recently, Judy's condition worsened, and although a rarity for her, she became depressed. Concealing her real situation, she kept insisting, "Don't worry, I'm fine. I'm managing." She was managing, but just barely. Lana and Evan read beneath the surface and decided to do something.

The call came:

> Mom, Lana and I have been talking, and we want to run this past you, so please listen and tell us how you feel. We have decided to move. With the kind of work I do, I can telecommute from anywhere. New York has always been special to us, and we want to move in with you. It's a big house. We will redesign it and take care of things so that you can do what you love and won't have to worry about the house. The kids adore you and so do we. We want to make things work for all of us. How does that sound to you?

Judy sobbed: "I can't believe it. It is so wonderful of you, a miracle come true." And so it was.

While this arrangement was positive for Judy, it may not work for you. Two families under a single roof, even under the best of circumstances, make for strain. Dissimilar lifestyles, different ages, varied personalities, diverse finances, competing needs and unlike interests can create challenges. Since life is dynamic and things can change, the trick is to see what is at stake and think it through. Make your choice carefully. It's your life.

OTHER HOUSING ALTERNATIVES

Some other options are senior housing, congregate housing, shared housing, assisted living, Continuing Care Retirement Communities (CCRC) and nursing homes. Within each of these categories, there may be a number of options and, given the enormity and growth of the "senior" market, more choices are emerging. The options available to your parent will depend on their functional abilities, finances and preferences. Be aware that not all seniors want to be only among seniors. At your family meetings, address housing now and housing in the future. And, if a change is needed, determine when the best time to move would be. Is it now or at a later date? Implicit in all of the decision making is the idea of "readiness." Sometimes, it just takes time.

For Beatrice, time was a big factor. Her move was impelled by major changes in the health of her family caregivers.

Beatrice: *Happy in the Nursing Home She Chose*

Ninety-two-year-old Beatrice resides in Arizona with her daughter, LuAnn, and son-in-law, Fred, where they all moved five years ago, when LuAnn and

Fred retired. Beatrice left New England, where she has another daughter and son-in-law, Enid and Ron, still actively working, and six grandchildren and three great-grandchildren.

Beatrice is frail. Her vision isn't so good anymore, nor is her hearing. She needs a walker to get around. She is being treated for several chronic conditions, including severe arthritis, and needs some help with bathing, dressing, medication management, meal preparation and transportation. All was well until three months ago when Fred was diagnosed with lung cancer. Shortly thereafter, LuAnn came down with a painful condition affecting her hands and feet and making it difficult to carry out her routine. One night, Beatrice fell and fractured her shoulder, necessitating more hands-on care. LuAnn and Fred, who were struggling with their own health issues, realized that they could no longer be her primary caregiver and she would be better off near the rest of the family. Calling Enid, Beatrice asked her to find a place, where she could live out her days comfortably, without making yet another move.

Enid and Ron invited her into their home, but she adamantly refused—did not want to be "a burden." Having already lived twenty-five years in retirement, she also was concerned about making her limited funds last. Enid and Ron now had homework to do—and quickly. They had to look into options such as assisted living and nursing homes and entitlements such as prescription assistance and Medicaid. Having spoken to several agencies and visited various facilities, they were still unsure. A geriatric care manager helped them put the information into perspective and develop and implement a plan.

Once a facility was chosen, Enid flew to Arizona to accompany her mother back East. Beatrice's cooperative attitude and her daughters' agreement made the pieces fit together like an easy-to-do puzzle. The family conference was accomplished by phone. The ability of the care recipient to participate in the planning process was a big plus. In this case, Beatrice consciously chose to enter a nursing home, where she is very happy.

THE LONG-DISTANCE CAREGIVER

What about the long-distance caregiver? If you're in one part of the country and your parent is in another and you cannot get on a plane immediately, what then? You might consider hiring a geriatric care manager to arrange for and supervise your parent's care and be the liaison with you.

If you or your parent are unable to pay for private care management services, entitlements like Medicaid and Veterans' benefit programs, or voluntary agencies such as church-based senior services and family service agencies, may offer assistance, so you can get things stabilized and do less flying. A good start would be to contact the Area Agency on Aging (Office for the Aging) in your parent's area to find out what is available and whom to contact. All areas are not equal. If there is a paucity of community resources for your parent, you may have to think about other options. These may include relocation to your area, where you can more easily arrange and supervise your parent's care.

TRANSPORTATION ISSUES

The importance of transportation for elders is often underestimated. If your parent cannot drive safely, whether due to failing eyesight or failing insight due to dementia, there needs to be a replacement mode of transportation, so that they can stay with their usual activities. Many areas have low-cost or no-cost vans that will take seniors to routine activities such as shopping, medical appointments or senior centers. These services are staffed by agency employees or community volunteers. Generally, arrangements must be made in advance, and sudden changes or urgent appointments cannot be accommodated, so there has to be a backup plan.

Reduced fares are available on public transport for those seniors able to travel this way. Many are reluctant or unable to use this mode. Some are afraid of the crowds of young people going to and from school, who though not intentionally, may be noisy and "scary." Others are fearful that even though the buses have wheelchair lifts, they don't always work. This would leave them waiting endlessly and feeling helpless. And individuals with dementia may become even more confused navigating public transportation.

What to do? You might think about hiring a part-time driver for your mom or dad's car or establishing a charge account with a local taxi service that they can access at any time. Although one can have one's personal auto at an Assisted Living Facility, local transportation is generally an included service, and many residents eventually give up their cars. Adult day health centers often come with transportation as an included service. Medical transportation, an ambulance for bed-bound individuals or an ambulette for the wheelchair bound can be costly and are not always covered by insurance. In some instances, it may be a necessary expense, nonetheless.

Dynamic, fluid and ever changing, care planning is a process. It takes time. It takes work. It takes energy. It takes love. It takes heart. Is it all worth it? Yes. You are making order out of chaos, identifying gaps and addressing them. In small or large ways, you are helping another and foreshadowing your own aging.

· 6 ·

Money, Money, Money

$\mathscr{F}$inances are a very sensitive subject for elders, and initiating a discussion about money may be difficult, if not impossible. Money is tied to security and independence and ultimately control. In addition to their own personal issues, some may have concerns about trusting their children with their finances, worrying that their money will not be there when they need it. Many will not relinquish the financial reins easily.

But, the fact is that information about your elder's financial status is important in determining how their everyday expenses will continue to be met and how added medical and long-term care costs could and should be handled. Planning ahead for long-term care should be given the highest priority. Access to their funds will be needed. Remember, this money is theirs and is to be used for their care and in their best interests.

GETTING ACCESS TO MONEY

Your parents saved for a rainy day. Well, it's pouring now, but they won't look out the window. They are not able to manage independently anymore and need care. You are trying to arrange it. You have discovered that the funds are there to make it possible, but you've also quickly realized that they have made no provision for you to get access. How do you get it?

First, if your parents are capable of understanding, you can try to ask. Sometimes that works. If they are agreeable, you now need Power of Attorney and whatever authorizing documents the banks, insurance companies and brokerage firms require. Now may be the time to engage a lawyer to draw up these documents. It also may be a good time to initiate some financial planning.

If care recipients no longer have the capacity to handle their own finances, who (a sibling or other designee) has been granted access to these funds, via a Power of Attorney or a joint account, for example? If there is no access, can a sibling or other relative advance needed monies until permanent arrangements can be made? If you do have to dig into your own funds, treat it as a loan and keep accurate records, so that repayment can be obtained. If the care recipient is unable to participate and there is no access to his or her funds, legal proceedings, such as Conservatorship or Guardianship, will have to be explored. A consultation with an attorney would be advisable.

If your parent resists, let some time pass. Try to ask again and again. Things may be very different on another day. Give it some time, but set a realistic deadline for when you need to get access. If things don't change, then it is time to consider legal action such as Conservatorship or Guardianship.

Your parents are barely getting along, trying to maintain their prior lifestyle. You can see that they are no longer managing their affairs appropriately even though a cloak of invincibility is maintained. They never saw any need for lawyers, accountants, financial planners or other unnecessary expenses. You finally realize that it's time for you to intervene, while it's still possible. Reluctantly, you step in.

Alfred and Zelda: Still Saving for a Rainy Day

"You never know what's going to happen. You have to save for a rainy day," says ninety-two-year-old Alfred, who still works every day in his own store and leaves work with cash in his pockets, walking past several banks as though they don't exist. "Never trusted them; never will." Carl, his only child, pleads with him: "Dad, times have changed. You could easily be mugged. You're a target. The banks are safe. And the IRS could come after you for some taxes." Carl is also anxious about his mother's failing health. She needs personal care and assistance, which she is not getting because Alfred is still saving for that "rainy day." There is no Power of Attorney granting Carl or anyone else authority to access the monies and the business in case of Alfred's incapacity, nor has there been financial or estate planning. Carl was able to convince Alfred to get legal and financial advice and was at his side through the process.

PAYING FOR HEALTH CARE

Medicare

Federally sponsored insurance for the elderly (over sixty-five), disabled (under sixty-five with certain disabilities) and those with end-stage renal disease (of all ages), Medicare is a program to pay for acute medical care. Medicare includes hospital insurance (part A), medical insurance (part B) and prescription drug coverage (part D). Part A covers most hospital bills, part-time and intermittent home care, a limited amount of nursing home care under specified circumstances, and hospice care. Part B covers most doctors' bills, medical equipment, outpatient care and diagnostic tests. Part D, newly established in 2006, covers prescription drugs. This benefit is accessed through a list of approved providers and can be confusing. The advantage is that it covers catastrophic medication expenses.

Many people erroneously believe that Medicare covers the cost of long-term care in a nursing home. In actuality, Medicare pays for only a limited amount of skilled care in a nursing home under certain conditions, such as for rehabilitation after a stroke or a joint replacement. A Medicare beneficiary must have had a (minimum) three-day hospital stay to qualify for nursing home services related to that hospitalization. Medicare does not pay for long-term custodial care. Since Medicare is a federal program, the rules are uniform from state to state.

All eligible enrollees are entitled to Medicare part A. Part B is optional, and subscribers who elect it pay a monthly premium that can be deducted from their Social Security payments. Part D is also optional and requires payment of a premium. In addition to the premiums, Medicare recipients are required to pay certain deductibles and copayments. Under part B, after payment of an annual deductible, Medicare generally pays 80 percent of its approved fees for eligible services. Medicare does not pay for eyeglasses and hearing aids. It pays only for specific preventive services such as flu and pneumonia vaccines and mammograms. Medicare beneficiaries can choose their health providers. Medicare information can be obtained from www.medicare.gov.

Medigap Policies

Medicare enrollees can purchase supplemental insurance policies (Medigap) from a private insurance company to cover the gaps in Medicare, such as the deductibles and copayments. While policies differ, a separate premium is required for this coverage, and it is guaranteed renewable as long as the premium is paid. Medigap policies are standardized and must follow federal and state laws. To buy a Medigap policy, an individual must have Medicare part A and part B in the original Medicare plan.

Medicare Managed Care

This is another option, in which beneficiaries may choose to enroll in a Medicare managed care program (Medicare Advantage plans), wherein they receive their Medicare benefits from an insurance company that is contracted with the federal government. Advantage plan members may or may not have to pay additional premiums to the insurance company. Managed care programs generally provide benefits similar to that covered by original Medicare. Included, too, may be additional benefits such as eyeglasses, hearing aids and routine physical examinations. However, they also may impose limitations that original Medicare does not. For example, you may be required to have a gatekeeper physician, from whom a specific referral is required for all tests, specialist care and hospitalizations. Be aware that choices are limited, and you may be restricted to using only specific hospitals, physicians, ancillary facilities and other providers. Medicare Advantage members may not purchase Medigap policies.

Program of All-Inclusive Care for the Elderly (PACE)

Another Medicare managed care option, the Program of All-Inclusive Care for the Elderly (PACE), is especially geared to nursing home–eligible, frail elderly who have both Medicare and Medicaid. Providing both acute and long-term care services, PACE is available in a limited but increasing number of states. It includes a comprehensive menu of services, emanating from a team of providers who are based in a center that houses a day-care program with medical and social services. In addition to the services at the center, home-delivered meals and home help are given to maintain the enrollee in the community. If nursing home care is required, this is offered, as well. PACE is an especially valuable resource for working caregivers.

PAYING FOR LONG-TERM CARE

Long-term care is expensive and can be a devastating expense, draining savings and other financial resources. While there is a substantial likelihood (43 percent) that after age sixty-five individuals will enter a nursing home at some point in their life, this figure can be misleading. At least half of the stays are short, three months or less; the other half, one year or more. It is the long stays that are potentially financially catastrophic.

Long-Term Care Insurance

Long-term care insurance is purchased by individuals who are concerned about the high cost of care, either in an institution or at home, and want to protect their assets. These policies are issued based on an applicant's health and age. Costs (premiums) are established accordingly. Policies are not available to individuals after a certain age or those already needing long-term care. This type of insurance varies in coverage and cost and may be expensive. Long-term care insurance is not for everybody but, rather, should be part of a rational financial plan, established well before the need for care arises. Long-term care insurance is not appropriate for those who are close to Medicaid eligibility.

Continuing Care Retirement Communities

The Continuing Care Retirement Community (CCRC) is another type of long-term care plan. This model combines housing, medical and social services in one community. As the residents' needs change, they can remain in the same community and receive appropriate care, ranging from independent living to long-term nursing home care. You may pay a sometimes substantial fee on entry and then defined monthly payments that enable you to access the care you need with predictable expenses. Contractual arrangements vary but can include refund of the entry fee to your estate. This option is well-suited to middle class persons with the assets and income to afford it, since they can enter a community, remain in it and get the services they need in a familiar environment and without financial devastation. It also helps couples with different levels of care needs to remain with or near each other. Costs range and individuals should locate communities that are affordable and appropriate for them.

Catastrophic Insurance

Where there is a long and expensive illness but no long-term care insurance, catastrophic insurance coverage may come into play for the relatively few individuals that have it. It behooves you, the caregiver, to have as much information as possible about your loved one's resources and benefits so you can evaluate the various options, based on both care needs and financial resources. When you are unsure of the availability of benefits such as long-term care or catastrophic insurance, and care recipients are unable to tell you, look at their records if you can access them or call their prior employer or union.

Veterans' Benefits

Veterans may be able to access low-cost health and even long-term care services. If your parent is a veteran, you should explore these benefits. General information about benefits and eligibility and the location of regional offices and Veterans Administration (VA) medical centers can be obtained by calling the

Department of Veterans Affairs at 800-827-1000. Some states also provide additional benefits that can be located through the local Office on Aging.

Medicaid

When the care recipient has very limited income and assets and requires long-term care services, either at home or in a nursing facility, Medicaid should be explored. The social worker at the hospital or the nursing home can provide information and referrals to appropriate agencies, as can the state or local Office on Aging or a private geriatric care manager.

Medicaid is the payer of last resort. It pays for medical services, including home health care and nursing home care for elders meeting its criteria for medical need, income and assets. If your care recipient has limited financial assets now, they may not meet the requirements until they "spend down" their assets to the point of eligibility. During that time, it is essential to keep good records regarding the expenditures that are made. Keep in mind that there are regulations about whether and to whom any monies or property can be transferred.

Information about how to apply can be obtained from the local Medicaid office in the local human resources administration or social services department. Documents and multiple years of financial records are required for an application. A family member should be involved. Since Medicaid is a federal program that is administered by each state, requirements and benefits vary from state to state or even area to area. Long-distance caregivers need to carefully investigate the differences between these benefits in the areas of interest if they are considering relocating their parents.

Where situations are complicated or unclear, caregivers may want to contact a lawyer who specializes in elder law. The local bar association may be a good source of referral. Also, the National Council of Elder Law Attorneys is located in Tucson, Arizona (602-881-4005).

REVERSE MORTGAGES: USING EQUITY IN THE HOME

A reverse mortgage is a loan that allows an older owner to use the equity value that has built up in their home without selling it or moving out of it. This may be an appropriate option for elders who are "house rich and cash poor," having considerable money invested in their home but not enough liquid assets (available money) to pay for health care, long-term care or even routine bills. The amount of money that can be received from a reverse mortgage depends on several factors, including the age of the elder, the amount of equity (wealth) in the home and the costs of the loan. When a reverse mortgage is obtained, the ownership of the home remains with the borrower, who is responsible for taxes and maintenance as always. Unlike other loans, the reverse mortgage does not obligate the borrower to make monthly payments. Rather, repayment of the loan and the interest become due when the borrower moves, sells the home or dies. With a reverse mortgage, the borrower can get the money in a lump-sum payment, a line of credit for use when needed or a regular monthly payment. Reverse mortgages do not affect eligibility for Social Security or Medicaid benefits.

There are variations in the amount of cash available, the terms of the loan and the total costs. All must be evaluated in considering this option, and wise consumers will consult their financial advisor as well as their family. A reverse mortgage is not the most appropriate option for everybody. And alternative options may exist for utilizing some of the equity value of your home such as refinancing your mortgage or obtaining a home equity loan.

INHERITANCE

Inheritance, the transfer of "wealth" between generations, is a thorny public policy issue. As a country, we are schizophrenic about inheritance. On the one hand, tax laws are skewed in the direction of the wealthy, enabling transfers and sheltering of assets for tax purposes. On the other hand, for those elders who require long term care and do not have adequate resources to pay for it, Medicaid policy is punitive about the transfer of assets. Medicaid is not intended to preserve anyone's inheritance.

Inheritance can turn out to be a difficult family issue, as well. Where there has been no planning and no discussion, family disputes tend to surface. Older adults need to get their financial "house in order" to avoid this. Financial awareness is a crucial part of eldercare planning.

While there are many people who may offer financial and legal tips and advice, it is advisable for the wise consumer to seek the advice of qualified, experienced legal and financial professionals. There are ever-changing rules and nuances that affect your parent's now situation and make it differ from that of friends or relatives who have done financial planning in the past. Inquire about professionals' fees. Note that their advice may even produce savings you never thought about.

PREVENTING FINANCIAL SCAMS AND EXPLOITATION

Elders are sometimes easy targets for financial scams. Their financial fears, coupled with their loneliness and diminished vision, hearing or insight make them easy prey. Often lured by promises of "easy fixes" for homes or cars or "easy money" from contests or investments, they are victimized and subject to substantial losses. Also, some are easily taken in by bogus telephone "charity" appeals. An older woman in the throes of early Alzheimer's disease had written donation checks for fifty thousand dollars before her family became aware.

While addressing financial issues, look for evidence of irregularities in the course of getting documents in order. For example, is there a disproportionate number of charity appeal letters lying around in piles? Are there unusual cash withdrawals and checks that cannot be explained? Have there suddenly been an abundance of house and car repairs? Have you noticed that valuables such as art, antiques and jewelry are no longer in place?

Listen to your intuition. If you have concerns, begin to address them. Sometimes, hard as you may try to protect your elder, they may resist, and it may take time before they will let you intervene. Don't give up. You, the caregiver, are there to assist and protect your elder. Remember, they have worked hard and saved diligently, and what they have is theirs. And you can only do as much as they will let you.

Of all the issues you face in eldercare planning, money may be the most contentious. Even in seemingly harmonious families, there can be sharp differences in the philosophies, beliefs, values, preferences, traits, experiences, feelings and lifestyles of the members. When it is time to plan strategies and expenditures, disagreements can develop, and it is best to resolve them at the first possible opportunity.

· 7 ·

Alzheimer's Disease

$\mathcal{A}$lzheimer's disease (AD) is the most common form of dementia in older adults. Centuries ago, dementia was the same as being crazy. Shakespeare, for example, used the term exactly this way. However, in recent times, the term has reemerged as meaning loss of intellectual functions such as remembering, thinking, reasoning and judgment, severe enough to interfere with daily life. Alzheimer's is a medical illness with behavioral symptoms that can mimic mental illness. Currently afflicting 4.5 million persons, its occurrence sharply increases with age. Affecting less than 1 percent of the population at age sixty-five, it affects as many as half of those over eighty-five. Not a normal part of aging, the course of AD is a long one, progressing from mild to moderate to severe dementia. A major public health issue today, the impact on the health-care system will increase dramatically, given the longevity boom we are experiencing.

Peter: The One and Only Caregiver

Peter and Tanya had a love affair, and the marriage that followed was a storybook romance. Peter had been widowed in his mid-forties and mourned as a loving, devoted husband. Some time after, a Russian family moved into the building, with an attractive, unmarried daughter in her thirties. Well-educated, her English was fluent. Love was instant, and their marriage produced two bright, handsome sons.

Continuing her career as a legal researcher throughout the marriage, Tanya took pride in uncovering the facts and remembering them all. In her early sixties, things began to change. Having difficulty doing her job, Tanya was forced to retire. Her problems became more and more obvious: short-term memory started to go downhill. Questions went on like a string with no end: "What time is it now? What time is it now? What time is it now?" "Are the boys coming tonight? Are the boys coming tonight? Are the boys coming tonight?" No longer able to dress herself, she looked bizarre when she attempted to: clothes didn't match, underwear was sometimes over her clothes and slippers were worn to go outside. With her playing with the stove, Peter was constantly turning it off, sniffing for gas fumes and scrupulously watching her every move. When Tanya wandered out of the house suddenly, Peter frantically searched until he found her, usually in the neighborhood somewhere, confused but undaunted. Soon thereafter, she became highly suspicious, accusing Peter of talking to the neighbors about her: "Why are you telling people that I'm crazy?" No amount of explanation soothed her. She also cried frequently. Not knowing what else to do, Peter consulted professionals. The diagnosis was Alzheimer's disease (AD).

Cringing upon hearing this, he went on the attack: "She just forgets," he burst out. "Who doesn't? We're all getting older, you know. And she's so, so sweet, such a gentle person and never hurts a soul. She dresses poorly; so what? She never was a fashion queen, but rather the intellectual I wanted. That's what makes it such a great marriage. We match."

The stranger her behavior, the more devoted he became and, though he did not admit it, the more depressed. Yet, that did not deter him. Professionals, friends, neighbors and family alike suggested assisted living for the two of them, pointing out that she would thrive where they had a special dementia unit, and he would have a life. Ignoring this, he became consumed with her care, and they clung to each other.

Their son, Boris, pleaded with him: "Dad, let us help you. We're not just worried about Mom. We're just as worried about you, in fact, more so. You used to play golf, go to the gym, go to the club, swim and do lots of things. Now you do nothing but take care of Mom, important as it is. And you're depressed as well. If you won't consider assisted living, at least get some help in the house—some relief for you." Furious, he would hear none of it: "Your mother is okay—not perfect, but we are managing. And no one is going to take care of her as long as I'm alive. No one. So, don't tell me what to do. I'm older than you and know what I'm doing. Now that you are both married, you would do the same. And your kids would never talk to you this way."

All the sons could do was visit and provide some change of routine for their mother in the moment, while watching their father provide smothering yet inadequate care. It was obvious that Tanya was losing weight and, while unintentional on Peter's part, was isolated and depressed. It was also clear that Peter's depression was going untreated and his health and social needs neglected.

PERSONS WITH AD AS INDIVIDUALS

Beginning subtly, AD progresses gradually, usually over a period of years. We must be aware that while the person is changing, at the same time they are retaining their personhood. People with AD are individuals and can't be painted with the same brush. Having different strengths and weaknesses, their symptoms may manifest differently. And they may have different amounts of reserve and ability to cover them over. Nonetheless, the basic needs for socialization, affection, control and fun remain long into the course of the illness.

Ed: The Horse Racing Enthusiast

Ed, an AD sufferer, was a racing enthusiast. As his AD progressed, things had to be modified so that he could continue to go to the racetrack frequently. No longer able to drive, he now had to be driven. As he became less and less able to deal with cash, his escort would guide him in his betting, along with giving him smaller bills to control his potential losses, since his judgment was poor. In this way, Ed was able to pursue his passionate hobby long into his illness.

Vera: Continuing Her Love for Dining Out

A good cook, Vera always liked dining in stylish restaurants. Now, in the middle stages of AD at age eighty-three, she still enjoys dining out. Unable to make proper choices from the menu, her daughter and son-in-law say, "You know what's terrific, Mom?" and do the ordering for her. Having been accustomed to use her credit card freely, Vera could no longer calculate the tip or add the numbers. In order not to hurt feelings or embarrass her, the daughter would take the card, when offered, saying, "I'll do it for you, Mom," and complete the transaction. Thus, Vera could continue her restaurant habit.

SYMPTOMS

Alzheimer's disease has a complex of symptoms that affect thinking, reasoning, judgment, everyday function, mood and behavior. The cognitive symptoms include declines in planning and organizing, short-term memory, language, judgment and orientation. The noncognitive symptoms include declines in the ability to perform basic daily activities and changes in personality, mood and behavior. Later in the course, there may be physical symptoms as well.

Cognitive Symptoms

Early on, there are difficulties with "executive function," planning and organizing complex tasks, even if they have been well-learned and routine. Tanya's inability to continue to do legal research, organize her findings and remember them is a poignant example. Everyday reasoning and problem-solving become problematic for the person who used to do it. Balancing a checkbook becomes impossible.

As with Tanya, short-term (recent) memory loss is a prominent sign that is always present. Occasionally forgetting your keys, leaving the gloves on the table or neglecting to turn the lights off as you leave are not necessarily Alzheimer's but probably your overprogrammed life. In AD, the memory impairment is not occasional but, rather, persistent and progressive, involving a decline from a prior level of function. AD is much more than forgetting. Tanya became unable to do the job that she had done for many years. Over time, she became unable to remember even the simplest information. Other examples follow: A practicing accountant with AD began missing tax deadlines. An actress noted for her fabulous memory started forgetting her lines. A railroad chef began missing his train.

Language disturbance is present. Difficulty finding the right words is symptomatic. Pointing to a shoe, the person says, "That's a pretty thing you have on your foot. What is it called again?" People with AD often start to say something and cannot remember how to finish the thought. They may have difficulty understanding what you are saying, and some cannot follow even the simplest directions. Eventually, they can lose their capacity to communicate.

Judgment is impaired. They may eat spoiled or moldy food or become unable to regulate the temperature of their bath or shower. They may step out of a moving car and cross the street against traffic. Or, unable to recognize the exploitation, they may become the victim of a scam. Loss of safety awareness—Tanya's playing with the stove, for example—can be dangerous and even life-threatening.

People with dementia cannot learn new things. When told something new, they cannot learn it and, therefore, cannot remember it. Learning to operate a new television or DVD player may not be possible, even for someone who was once savvy about technology. This is also true regarding learning their way around new places, such as a new residence.

Confusion

AD causes confusion: "What am I supposed to do now?" There is also disorientation to time, place and person: "Where are we?" And standing in their bedroom, they might say, "I want to go home." Months and years may also be scrambled or unknown: "What day is it today?" Familiar places may no longer be familiar to them. And they may not recognize people they know, even their own spouses and children. These symptoms must be distinguished from delirium, an acute-onset mental change that includes extreme confusion, fluctuating consciousness and attention, and sometimes hallucinations. Delirium can be a life-threatening emergency, related to medical illness.

Changes in Function

There is a decline in the ability to perform the Activities of Daily Living (ADL)—bathing, dressing, toileting, eating, transferring (from sitting to standing or getting in and out of bed) and walking. Usually, bathing and dressing are the earliest ADL losses. When Tanya looked bizarre, it was because of this. Before her illness, she always dressed appropriately and would never have worn her bedroom slippers outside. This would have horrified her. Because people with AD eventually lose their ability to perform their ADLs, they require the assistance of others to survive.

Physical Symptoms

Some individuals develop signs that resemble Parkinson's disease. These people may have Lewy Body Disease, medication side effects, or Parkinson-like symptoms, usually developing later in the course of AD. Other physical issues can include disturbances in gait and balance that may make the patient more prone to falling, difficulty controlling muscle movements, and problems walking or swallowing.

Personality Changes

Personality may remain as it always was or change dramatically. Someone who was mild can become ferocious. A polite person may begin to curse in expletives. Someone who was assertive and demanding can turn withdrawn and submissive. A pussycat turned into a lion and the lion a pussycat. These personality changes sometimes are embarrassing for family members. On a bus or train, an AD mother may turn to her daughter seated beside her and loudly protest, "Where the f—— are you taking me?" or, "Look at that fat woman over there."

Changes in Mood and Behavior

AD sufferers can show changes in mood and behavior. Depression may precede dementia, develop simultaneously or come afterward. There is also a condition called "pseudodementia," which looks like dementia but is, in fact, depression or anxiety and can fool even the professionals. People with AD may cry frequently, as did Tanya, become withdrawn or have wide mood swings. One moment, they are ecstatic, the next, sad. Additionally, they may become fearful, angry or suspicious. Tanya accused Peter of telling the neighbors "she is crazy." Wandering, sleeplessness, agitation, resistance to care, apathy and, sometimes, aggression are other dementia-associated behaviors. AD, with its related behavioral problems, is the most common trigger for nursing home placement in the United States.

Wandering

Wandering is a behavior that is especially scary. Why people wander is unknown and whether and when they will is unpredictable. To assume that they will not wander because they haven't already wandered is an unsafe assumption. Prevention is important. How? First, individuals with AD should have an identification bracelet spelling out their memory loss and any medical problems. The Alzheimer's Association has Project Safe Return (800-272-3900), "a nationwide identification, support and registration program that provides assistance, whenever a person is lost locally or far from home." There are also various medical identification programs that include a twenty-four-hour emergency number through which caregivers can be contacted. Securing appropriate identification jewelry is an essential first step. Second, wanderproof the house. Equip doors and windows, as appropriate, with an alarm or complicated locks that the AD sufferer cannot work, to alert the caregiver before the wanderer gets too far. Third, in addition to wanderproofing, implement safety measures in the house, so that when the care recipient wanders aimlessly, the likelihood of getting hurt is minimized. Specifically, get rid of clutter so that there is a clear path; remove loose throw rugs; keep gates at tops and bottoms of stairways; lock basement doors (through which a confused elder could access steps to fall down); and remove from visibility hazardous objects, such as poisonous cleaning materials, knives and scissors, weapons, matches, car keys and medications. Shut off the stove with a valve or remove the knobs when the stove is unsupervised.

Resistance to Care

Aside from wandering, which causes great anxiety, the most difficult behavior is resistance to care: care recipients will not change their clothes, refuse to take a bath or shower, will not allow you to dress them or refuse their medications. Whatever you try to do, they thwart you. Know that you are not alone. Helpful tips may be available from other caregivers who are experiencing the same issues, such as members of a support group. Your care team is also knowledgeable in this regard.

Sleeplessness

Sleeplessness is another big challenge, especially if you, the caregiver, have obligations that you must do each morning, such as getting to your job or getting the children off to school. If your care recipient has an overlay of depression, the depression may be causing or contributing to the insomnia, and treatment of the depression may alleviate this. In the mid- to later stages of AD, the sleep cycle can be disturbed, and your care recipient may mix up days and nights. Sometimes, sleeplessness responds to medications. A combination of strategies is best, including keeping the patient busy during the day, so that there is a clear distinction between day and night; limiting naps; cutting down on caffeine late in the day; using a night-light to lessen confusion and anxiety; and encouraging a consistent sleep routine.

A PARADOX BETWEEN APPEARANCE AND FUNCTION

Individuals with AD generally look okay, no visible signs apparent. With cancer, for example, there are noticeable periods of illness and pain. With heart disease, symptoms such as shortness of breath or leg edema (swelling) are visible. With a fracture, there is pain and immobility. But with AD, at least until the more advanced stages, there are no obvious physical symptoms amid the subtle mental and functional changes that are happening. It is, thus, hard to accept that afflicted individuals are really sick. If Tanya was sitting with visitors after Peter had dressed her and she stayed quiet and smiling, no one would have noticed her illness. This paradox between appearance and function is unique to AD. At the same time, it is acutely disquieting for both families and professionals alike.

WHAT CAUSES AD?

The cause of AD is still unknown. While the central problem appears to be the death of nerve cells in the brain (neurons), the reasons for this are uncertain. Possible explanations include abnormal biochemical processes, inflammation and genetic components. Experts believe that a combination of factors is involved, rather than a single cause. The greatest known risk factor at this time is advanced age. Family history is another strong influence. Having an affected blood relative can increase the risk. Genetic aberrations have been uncovered. Abnormal chromosomes have been identified in a small proportion of cases, and these are being studied vigorously. Having the Apolipoprotein E4 (ApoE4) gene has been identified as a risk factor—it plays a role but having it doesn't necessarily mean that AD is a certainty. Scientists are now investigating lifestyle factors such as intellectual stimulation, diet, exercise and stress and their impact on brain health.

OTHER CONDITIONS CAUSING DEMENTIA

While all individuals with AD have dementia, all individuals with dementia do not have AD. There are myriad conditions that cause symptoms of dementia or mimic them. Among these are alcoholism, drug abuse, drug reactions or interactions, metal poisoning, severe vitamin deficiency, strokes, brain tumors, infections, metabolic abnormalities, head trauma and other neurological diseases.

Related dementing illnesses include Lewy Body Disease, Normal Pressure Hydrocephalus (NPH), multi-infarct dementia, Creutzfeldt-Jakob Disease (CJD), Pick's disease and Parkinson's. Lewy Body Disease has symptoms that are a combination of Alzheimer's and Parkinson's. Normal Pressure Hydrocephalus is caused by an obstruction in the flow of spinal fluid. Multi-infarct dementia is caused by multiple strokes (infarcts) in the brain and is also known as vascular dementia. Vascular dementia may occur independent of Alzheimer's or in combination with it. Creutzfeldt-Jakob Disease is caused by infection. Pick's, although rare, resembles Alzheimer's, but personality changes and aberrant behaviors may precede the memory loss. Parkinson's affects motor function, while AD affects cognitive function; however, in later stages, dementia can occur.

A medical work-up for the diagnosis of Alzheimer's disease must include systematic elimination of other possible causes. This is especially important since some of these conditions are reversible, whereas AD is not.

WHO GETS AD?

AD is a very democratic disease, affecting people of all ethnicities and socioeconomic groups, although women may be at higher risk than men. Generally, people with AD are over sixty-five, most being in their seventies, eighties and above. However, younger people, in their thirties, forties and fifties can be affected, too (early onset), but this is rare and accounts for only 10 percent of all cases.

DIAGNOSING AD

At this time, there is no single diagnostic test for Alzheimer's. Rather, AD is a diagnosis made on the basis of a comprehensive work-up that includes at least a detailed medical history, a mental status assessment, a thorough physical examination, a neurological examination, a series of blood tests, electrocardiogram (EKG), brain imaging (CT, MRI, or PET or SPECT) and possibly electroencephalogram (EEG)—neuropsychological testing and psychiatric evaluation. A thoughtful clinical diagnosis based on this data may be up to 95 percent accurate. Definitive diagnosis is generally made by postmortem examination (autopsy) or, rarely, by brain biopsy. A large proportion of individuals with AD, perhaps 25 percent, remain undiagnosed.

TREATING AD

Although there is no medical treatment at this time to cure or stop the progression of AD, there is an increasing body of knowledge about management. The goal is to slow the progression of this long-term devastating illness and optimize the quality of life. Several drugs may temporarily improve the symptoms. Additionally, medications are available to manage associated behavioral symptoms, such as depression, agitation and sleeplessness. Nonpharmacologic and alternative approaches are being tried as well. These include exercise, acupuncture, nutritional interventions such as a "brain healthy" diet, vitamin supplements and training of family caregivers. Specialized support groups are available for individuals with early AD.

Intensive research is underway to better understand the mechanisms of the disease and find treatments to slow and eventually cure it. Additionally, there are efforts to develop preventive strategies. Most encouraging is the fact that more progress has been made in studying AD in the past two decades than in the first eighty years since its description by Dr. Alois Alzheimer.

Since AD is a condition that lasts over the long haul, attention must be paid to the maintenance of the general health and safety of the patient, in order to maintain quality of life. Older individuals with AD may have other coexisting health issues that require management as well—high blood pressure, diabetes, heart abnormalities, arthritis or chronic pain. Left untreated, these can confound and compound the dementia. And falls and accidents that impede mobility contribute to significant declines in daily comfort.

AD AND SERVICE USE

Over the course of the illness, the affected individual may use a changing spectrum of services. Early on, there may be attendance at the local senior center. When this is no longer feasible, attendance at an adult day health program is appropriate. Some at-home personal care is helpful. From time to time, respite for the primary family caregiver is strongly suggested.

There's no one universal plan. Different patients have different backgrounds and interests. People who have worked all their life may see a senior center or a day health center as ridiculous and childlike. For them, work was their leisure and leisure was work, and they knew nothing else. It is best if this can be accommodated. Fortunately, in this case, it could.

Charlie: "The Office" as Day Care

Charlie had started his own construction business, eventually bringing in other family members, including his three sons. With the advent of his illness, of necessity, his sons took over. However, sensitive to his feelings of powerlessness and loss, they arranged for him to go to work each day. Driven by one of his sons, he had a desk and a phone and shared one son's secretary, the latter having been counseled as to how to work with him: she gave him mail to open, gave him plans to look at, planned sites to visit with his son, arranged lunch dates with family and friends and accompanied him at all times. This was, in effect, his day care—tailored for him. With this in place, things went along well for about two years, when Charlie's condition changed and he needed more care.

ASSISTED LIVING OR NURSING HOME?

As the severity of dementia increases and caregiving becomes more challenging, placement in a health-care facility may be the best option. Historically, nursing homes have been the primary setting for institutional care. However, more and more, families are placing individuals with AD in assisted living facilities instead of nursing homes. Assisted living facilities have had an explosive growth in the last decade or so and provide care for substantial numbers of individuals with dementia. Still, nursing homes remain an important service for some.

What is right for your loved one? There are few differences, except that assisted living facilities may have more difficulty handling individuals with complex or unstable medical or nursing needs and are inclined to hospitalize these residents more frequently. (Criteria for selecting Assisted Living Facilities are presented in chapter 8, as is information about dementia-specific units.)

In the moderate stages of AD, when individuals are ambulatory and need cueing, supervision, personal care and a highly structured day, assisted living can meet their needs. And, if a single room is important, it may be able to provide this more readily than a nursing home. However, as the disease progresses and the individuals require more hands-on care and nursing supervision, the better answer may be a nursing home. Areas of care that are important include management of behavioral symptoms, treatment of depression, assurance of optimal food and fluid intake, provision of activities and efforts to promote their continuing to walk. For later-stage individuals, special attention should be paid to swallowing abilities, prevention of skin breakdown (bedsores), and optimal food and fluid intake.

COSTS OF LONG-TERM CARE

Costs vary among facilities and even within a facility, according to the level of care needed. And there may be additional charges beyond the daily rate. The good consumer will study these and take them into account. Further, some entitlement programs will fund one level of care but not another. For example, while Medicaid will pay for assisted living in some states but not others, it will pay for nursing home care in all states.

Sources of information include the facilities (ask to see an admission agreement), members of your support group, the local chapter of the Alzheimer's Association and Office on Aging, your state's health department, your parent's physician or a geriatric care manager. Whichever place you select, be clear also on their policies regarding transfer to another facility when care needs change or when the resident runs out of funds.

HOSPICE CARE FOR INDIVIDUALS WITH DEMENTIA

Hospice care can be beneficial to individuals in the final stages of AD and other dementias and their families. Hospice includes palliative (comfort) care for the patient and bereavement counseling and support for family members. Hospice patients or their surrogates choose to forgo aggressive life-sustaining treatments such as cardiopulmonary resuscitation, antibiotics and artificial feeding and hydration. Since AD patients may be unable to communicate their pain, careful assessment and management of pain are important care components. Individuals can receive hospice care in their home, in a free-standing hospice facility, in assisted living or in a nursing home.

Because it can be difficult to identify AD patients who have a life expectancy of six months or less (per hospice criteria), some hospice programs have rules specific to individuals with dementia. Hospice providers are not all the same, so you might choose the one in your area that is most "dementia friendly."

AD IS A FAMILY AFFAIR

Eighty percent of the care of individuals with AD is provided by families, who have been called the "secondary victims" or "hidden victims." Like all family members, Peter, the husband we met earlier, was pulled into a system over which he had little control. Not knowing where they came from or where they were going, he had to handle his wife's symptoms. His own turmoil, swirling within him, was pushed aside by the everyday realities of Tanya's needs. The only way he could handle the tumult was to cloak himself in denial. While denial is not uncommon, nor is it necessarily dangerous in itself, when it interferes with reality and sound decision making, it can turn into a serious problem. Denying the vulnerability we all experience, he swung to the other side, using an armor of invincibility to survive. He could do all, see all, be all and feel all for Tanya—and himself.

CAREGIVER DEPRESSION

Truth be told, caregivers are not invincible. In fact, due to the stress they undergo, they are more prone to illness. Additionally, neglect of their personal needs confounds this. Peter stopped socializing, exercising and paying attention to his own health needs. And, of course, his denial prevented him from acknowledging his own depression. His sons, understandably, were extremely concerned about this.

Depression is rampant in AD caregivers and often makes them the second patient in the mix. Peter is by no means alone in this. Loss being the underpinning of depression, he was losing Tanya day by day and inch by inch. The Tanya he had known was no longer the Tanya in front of him. Feeling helpless, he just swooped down on her, as though becoming a part of her would make her whole again. In actuality, he was losing ground. Parts of him were disappearing as well. And nothing he could do seemed to make a difference. He felt impotent.

He, the competent attorney, to whom everyone had turned for advice, the one who would appear in court and charm a jury, who could sympathize with the victim and win a case against all odds, had lost his clout. As an attorney, he had been a team player, working with other attorneys, secretaries, paralegals, expert witnesses and judges. Now he was a lone isolate, feeling like the savior and the victim, both at the same time. And neither one felt right. For Peter, the dramatic change of roles and lifestyle were traumatic. Yet, he made no effort to enlist any help or make any changes.

SHRINKING SOCIAL NETWORKS

Becoming a caregiver was involuntary and isolating. Social supports shrank, eventually becoming almost nonexistent. While outwardly people applauded him for being "self-sacrificing, wonderful, a hero, a fantastic husband and a selfless human being," there was no real people contact. Friends and neighbors stayed away, since being near him and Tanya made them feel helpless. They didn't know what to do, either.

Compounding the shrinking social supports for many caregivers is the fact that, as the disease progresses, communication becomes more impaired, and the care recipient eventually becomes unable to provide any feedback. Thus, unlike other diseases, there's little chance of closure with AD, but rather there's the "long goodbye" without an end.

FAMILY RELATIONSHIPS

AD does not affect only the person involved. Its tentacles affect everyone in the family. No one escapes. In Peter and Tanya's case, the sons were conflicted. Who would not be? They loved their mother. They loved their father. Part of them wanted to visit; part of them did not. "These are my parents. I need to be there for them. I will do it, no matter how bad I feel." Once actually there, while wanting to run, they don't. They really feel like saying, "Dad, we know you're doing the best you can and how hard it is for you, but we think Mom needs more assistance, more stimulation and an environment that is less isolating. And it's just not happening." Knowing how defensive he would be, they say none of this. Instead, it gnaws inside of them. Aware that, at this point, they can do nothing, powerless, they stand on the sidelines, waiting for the inevitable crisis to happen.

THE CAREGIVER, THE CARE RECIPIENT AND THE DISEASE

AD is tough on families. It doesn't matter whether someone is a child or a spouse, a hands-on caregiver or the relative of an individual who has been placed, the situation can be overwhelming. For some family members, it gets tougher in the more advanced stages; for others, it seems to get easier. Everybody handles it differently. Support groups are available for caregivers to share their experiences and get practical tips and emotional support.

Clem: Searching for Reasons

Clem is the forty-nine-year-old son of Gladys, who just turned seventy-eight. A resident of a nursing home for the last three years, Gladys has severe dementia: cannot bathe, dress, groom, toilet, transfer or walk independently and needs to be hand-fed. An attractive woman, she always made a weekly trip to the beauty salon and now has her hair and nails done in the facility's beauty shop. She is always dressed in well-coordinated clothing. While living in her own world most of the time, it is a happy world. Generally smiling, she frequently sings and laughs. Personnel, accustomed to caring for individuals with dementia, know that her kicking, screaming and pulling their hair while they try to perform personal care are not deliberate acts of aggression but rather part of her disease. Appreciating her usually happy demeanor, they forgive the outbursts.

Clem, a high school teacher, has not been able to come to terms with his mother's disease. Frightened by her dementia and the associated aggressive behaviors, he seldom visits. When he does, he always finds his mother "worse." "She doesn't know what's going on. She spits her food out. Like an animal, she claws at the staff, yells and carries on—even bites when they get too close. I've told my wife to take a gun and shoot me if I ever get like that."

Looking for a rationale and covering over his own feelings of revulsion, Clem seeks to project it all out onto the world: "She wouldn't be in this dehumanized state if only the staff did their jobs better, the doctors prescribed the right medications, her diet was improved and there were more people for her to talk to." Underneath all of this searching for reasons is the real reason: the terror that he, one day, will be just like this, a haunting nightmare that never leaves. While no other close relative has been afflicted and there is, therefore, no reason to suspect any rampant genetic pattern, the haunting terror lives inside him.

What can Clem do? Clem can choose to suffer with the terror or confront it. There are treatment options for caregivers, including support groups, caregiver training, individual counseling, group therapy and possibly medications. Treatment can help to reenergize his life and restore his capacity for pleasure.

Peg: Struggling to Maintain the Status Quo

Peg, a nurse, never married, shares a home with her mother, Joan. Mother and daughter were always close and became even closer when her mother became a widow eight years ago, at age sixty-seven. Each self-sufficient, they also enjoyed spending time with each other. Joan, a secretary in a public school, retired at seventy-one. Peg works in a nursing home that has an adult day health center.

Five years ago, Joan began to show the beginning signs of AD. Peg noticed them right away. Taking her mother to a Memory Center, she was told that it was, indeed, AD and was given all the updated information available. Sharing this with her two older sisters, they were unfazed and would take no responsibility for their mom. Obviously, she was now "it." All three went to see an eldercare lawyer. Ultimately, everything was to be split equally, except the work.

For the first three years after the diagnosis, Joan was able to stay alone during the day, be escorted to the nearby senior center and visit with family and friends. Then there was a more noticeable downhill slide: Joan could no longer be left alone; she became incontinent of urine, delusional and aggressive. Peg arranged to take Joan to the adult day health program at her facility three days a week, for one sister to take her one day a week, for the other sister to cover another day and for Peg to remain at home with her mother the rest of the time. With a change of heart, all the daughters were trying their best, but things were chaotic.

Although she was cared for, Joan's schedule lacked a consistent structure, fostering anxiety. The more anxious she became, the more confused she became—and ever more difficult to manage: "What are you trying to do to me, keep me away from my home?" Distraught and angry, she burst out in a menacing tone, "You're not the daughter I used to know. And, don't worry. I have ways of handling that. You'll find out." Peg did find out. Shortly thereafter, as Peg was trying to comb her mother's hair, Joan suddenly lunged at her and tried to choke her. Horrified, Peg yanked Joan's hands off her neck and moved out of reach. Some time later, feeling totally inadequate, she confided to her best friend: "There I was. My loving, sweet mother was trying to kill me. Imagine? Here I am—literally killing myself trying to help her, and there she is trying to kill me. Can you believe it?"

Behavioral disturbances such as these, as awful as they are, are not unusual in the later stages of AD. And these are probably the most common reasons that family caregivers seek placement outside the home. With this need for placement comes great difficulty with decision making: grief over the loss of the loved one they once knew, guilt over not being able to handle the responsibilities they undertook and a sense of failure.

> I always felt responsible for my mother's care. But, no matter how hard I tried, she didn't get better. In fact, she got worse. Though she raged at me, I feel it was I who let her down. Much as I understand that I need to

place her, emotionally, I can't bring myself to do it. While the administrator of the facility where I work is willing to accept her and make necessary financial arrangements so that I can maintain my work schedule with a clear head, I'm still in conflict. It all seems so final, and I guess I'm just not ready for it. Strange, I can help other families who bring their relatives to my facility, but when it comes to my own mother, I'm stuck.

Like all illnesses, AD is a complex of symptoms. But, unlike many other conditions, it is long term, variable and unpredictable. Yet, on a human level, it is a very personal experience for all involved, including you, the caregiver. Were you to stay stuck, you would remain immobilized—inefficient, deenergized, demoralized and generally unable to cope. But, you are coping and doing a phenomenal job. Maybe you're making it up as you go along, but that's part of the job, and in so doing, you are participating in your own growth experience. Indeed, there is light in the darkness of this disease and it is you who are carrying it.

8

The Road to Placement

Place my mother? What are you talking about? How could I
ever do such a thing to her? I would feel like a monster. And
everybody else would see me the same way.

—A support group member

$\mathcal{P}$lacement is not usually the first choice. Despite what everybody thinks,
families struggle to keep the disabled older person at home for as long as
possible, and sometimes even past that. While there's stereotypical thinking
about the older person sitting in front of a television screen in a nursing home,
the truth is that on any given day, the overwhelming majority of elders live at
home. And they are cared for by family. By the time placement is considered,
things are spinning out of control.

NURSING HOMES: A BRIEF HISTORY

Nursing home care is stigmatized and probably always was. As far back as
the Middle Ages when longevity was not in vogue, older persons without
families to care for them were housed in almshouses. More poor than necessarily sick or disabled, they had to work for their keep—making their own
beds, raising the animals, helping out in the kitchen, doing laundry and
keeping the place running. Over time, small "mom and pop" nursing homes
developed. A household having a nurse was now taking in a few people to
care for.

We will fast-forward to the mid-twentieth century and the birth of
Medicare and Medicaid: the nursing home industry now had the funding
to develop and boom. In addition to the mom and pop–owned places, large

investor-owned chains of facilities emerged. With this boom came problems. Scandals made the headlines from time to time. And all too often, care was poor. Most hands-on care was provided by the least trained staff. Residents were not properly evaluated, restraints were often used in place of care, abuse was overlooked, resident rights were minimized and mental health problems were left untreated. Staff was not screened for criminal backgrounds or a history of patient abuse. These issues were addressed by corrective legislation passed in the late 1980s and early 1990s.

Further, with the graying of the population and the potentially explosive numbers of elders, increasing attention was focused on nursing homes and other long-term care services. More physician and nurse specialization and certification programs in geriatrics and gerontology were developed. Nursing homes became more integrated into medical practice.

Today, nursing homes care for the frailest and sickest elderly. While the socioeconomic status of nursing home residents is varied, about one-half of nursing home days nationally are paid for by Medicaid. Medicare does not pay for long-term custodial care; rather, only short-term stays for rehabilitation, certain equipment such as special wheelchairs and supplies such as wound care necessities are covered. While most residents are not necessarily poor on admission, it often takes only a matter of months for many to exhaust their life's savings and become eligible for Medicaid. About one-third of nursing home residents have stays of less than six months, another third, six months to two years, and the remaining one-third, more than two years.

MONITORING QUALITY OF CARE

Highly regulated, there is more surveillance of nursing homes than ever before. Systems are in place for monitoring indicators of poor care such as pressure sores (bedsores), falls with injuries, inappropriate medications, restraint use, fecal impaction, inadequate pain management and unexpected declines in function.

Assessment of residents is required on admission and at specified intervals thereafter. A minimum amount of initial training is compulsory for the certification of nursing aides, along with annual continuing education credits. Facilities are mandated to have a Quality Assurance program. Every facility must have a designated medical director. States and organizations post report cards on the Internet, and each facility is required to post its survey results conspicuously. Despite the fact that there have been so many corrective changes in nursing home practice, there remains lots of room for improvement.

MAKING THE DECISION

Placing your parent is the most painful decision you will have to make. Why? First, your parent may not want to go and may be very vocal about it. "You're sending me to a nursing home? You want me to die? Haven't I been a good enough parent? Why don't you just throw me away?" So, now you are bombarded with feelings of guilt shooting through you. Second, you, the caregiver, are ambivalent and filled with doubt. "Have I really done enough? Is there something else I can try?"

You, the caregiver, consumed by these emotions, have to set them aside and deal with the situation in a logical, sane and protective way. Carefully appraise your loved one's condition. Here are some specifics to explore: can he or she bathe, dress and groom themselves; use the toilet independently; get in and out of a chair or a bed safely; walk independently; get and prepare food; feed her- or himself; handle medications; and find opportunities for socializing? If you've answered "no" to most of the above, your elder relative's state of independence is precarious. Take a deep breath and ask yourself the cutting question, "How much of this help am I really able to provide?"

Here's some more for you to think about: If your parent were to be kept at home, is the home a good fit? How much care would be needed? Can a safe and realistic plan be initiated? What would that cost? Where would that money come from? How long would it last? What happens when the money runs out?

PAYING FOR CARE AT HOME

Medicare generally pays for intermittent care for homebound persons who meet specified criteria. Skilled services such as nursing, physical therapy and occupational therapy are provided at home, as well as very limited amounts of aide services. In general, Medicare does not pay for "custodial services"—supervision, personal care, meal preparation and housekeeping. With required evidence of a medical as well as financial need, Medicaid will pay for these services. However, most elderly persons pay privately for home health care, hiring their own individuals or employees of home health agencies, voting with their pocketbooks and their feet to remain in their own homes, rather than seek placement.

ARRANGING FOR AT-HOME CARE

If you feel that home care is the way to go, you need to locate a funding source. If your elder qualifies for Medicaid, then an assessment will be performed and a care plan developed by Medicaid personnel. If, on the other hand, your elder has funds available to pay for it, then your next step is to develop a home-care plan: Specifically what services is an aide needed to provide? How many hours of care does your relative actually require on a daily basis? To decide this, caregivers must figure out how many hours at a time their relatives can be left alone safely. Does being by themselves at night present a danger? Consider the following: Are they likely to wander outdoors? Have they fallen? Can they find their way around the house? Can they call for help in an emergency? Can they safely leave the house independently for socialization and activities, such as at senior centers, religious services, cultural events, medical appointments and beauty services? If so, what form of transportation is needed? If they are more frail, an adult day health center, which provides socialization, meals, supervision and transportation, may be a good complement to limited home care.

FINDING HOME CARE

If you have determined that your relative does not require full-time help, then you would be looking for an hourly worker. On the other hand, if your relative requires constant supervision, you need a round-the-clock aide. This can be done in different ways: with full-time, live-in help, two or three daily shifts or a family member part-time, supplemented by hired help. To locate outside help, you might contact a home health agency that is licensed in your area and possibly certified by Medicare, as well. You would be seeking either a Certified Home Health Aide (CHHA) or a Certified Nursing Assistant (CNA). Agencies generally perform reference checks and background checks and also offer assessment and supervision by a Registered Nurse (RN). Some handle the payroll and the taxes. Ask about these services. Others charge a finder's fee up front. And you are responsible for the rest. Alternatively, you may find an individual through a private referral by a family member, neighbor or friend and may perform background and reference checks. Not only are you interested in their paper qualifications but also their personal qualities such as compassion, warmth and kindness. In all of this, someone must be in charge, a household manager and supervisor. A family member usually does this, when the frail elder is no longer able to. Daunting? Yes. Necessary? Yes.

Before you rule out home care, there are other alternatives: you can hire a professional geriatric care manager to set it up and oversee it all. This is a relatively new type of service, coming about as a result of the aging explosion, the pressures of the "sandwich generation" and the fact that most adult children are working. Along with this is the heightened geographic mobility that creates a lot of long-distance caring. While they can't always be there on the moment, adult children do want to assure that their older parents are cared for.

Some states offer at-home nursing home alternatives that are generally funded through special Medicaid waivers. The elder, who meets financial and medical criteria, remains at home, where he or she receives a menu of different services. While these programs are an expansion of traditional home care, they generally do not provide twenty-four-hour custodial services and thus are more suitable for elders who do not live alone.

IS HOME CARE FOR EVERYONE?

You may want to. Your parent may want you to. Your siblings may want you to. The neighbors may want you to. Your heart is pushing you to do it, but what is the reality? Can you really pull it off?

Caring for an elder at home is, by no means, a static situation. You have to be vigilant all the time and ready for change on a moment's notice. Your father's aide has called to say that she can't find him. He must have wandered while she was in the shower. Where do you look? Whom do you call? Or, Mom's aide has a family emergency, and she has to leave for another state—now. Having been with you for many months, there are no substitutes waiting in the wings. Or, Mom's condition has had a radical shift, and she needs to get to the Emergency Room. Pronto, you have to get there, too. Another example follows: The kitchen faucet springs a leak and has suddenly become a waterfall. The aide cannot turn it off, and no one is around to help her. Who can drop everything and run?

Home care can be as expensive as facility-based care, or even more so. For instance, if your care recipient has developed an irregular sleep pattern, as in the later stages of dementia, and requires round-the-clock supervision and assistance, you may be forced to use shifts of care (two twelve-hour or three eight-hour), paying for each and every hour, rather than using live-in help. Or, if the care recipient is "dead weight" or very heavy, at times they may require a second person for lifting and transferring, which also can increase the costs.

While placement may not have been your priority choice, now knowing the complexities of home care, you may need to reconsider.

RECONSIDERING: WHAT DO I DO NOW?

The time has come; the choice has been hard, but placement is on the horizon. What type of facility would best suit your loved one's needs? When people think about facilities, the first thought that pops into their head is—nursing home. That used to be the case. But no longer is it so. There are various types of facility-based care, each providing a different configuration of services. What are these different kinds?

Boarding homes, group homes, residential care facilities and assisted living facilities are generally appropriate for individuals who do not have ongoing, skilled medical needs such as twenty-four-hour on-site nursing, complex special diets or wound care for severe pressure sores. The names of these levels of care and the services offered may differ from state to state. Some facilities cater to specific conditions such as Alzheimer's disease, chronic psychiatric problems or traumatic brain injuries. They differ in size and cost. Some are smaller and more homelike than the typical nursing home. They vary widely in level of staffing and services provided but may be a good option for those preferring a smaller environment. Also, the costs may be less, an attractive feature for families with limited funds. While coverage for stays in some facilities may be provided by some entitlement programs (Medicaid, disability funding or respite), this varies from state to state.

Continuing Care Retirement Communities (CCRC) are providers of multiple levels of "life care" for their occupants. These levels, usually in a campus setting, include independent living, assisted living, home care, nursing home care and hospice, and some also have their own medical staff and clinics. While some of these facilities are quite upscale, others are more moderate, and the costs vary. The advantage of the CCRC is that the residents are able to avail themselves of a spectrum of care in a community that is familiar and can accommodate their changing care needs. Also, a couple with very different care needs can be maintained in the same community, making it easy for the well spouse to have access to the ill spouse. The fees do not necessarily rise commensurate with increasing care needs. This is made possible by sometimes substantial entry fees that are used to capitalize and subsidize the operations. This is a good option when your parent is healthier. Because the CCRC is just like insurance, certain preexisting conditions may be excluded. And by the time an individual needs a nursing home, it's too late for this option.

ASSISTED LIVING

Assisted living is housing enmeshed with services. Unlike nursing homes, where there is a panoply of services available to every resident, assisted living is more of an a la carte menu, where one can pick and choose only those services that are needed, with the fees determined by the services needed. Assisted living facilities may be freestanding or part of a campus with a continuum of care. They may be individually owned or part of a chain of corporate-owned facilities. Sponsorship may be for-profit or nonprofit.

The elder resides in a suite or small apartment, shared or not shared, and receives a basic package of services including housekeeping, meals, nursing supervision, activities and transportation to physicians, religious services and outside events. Additional services can be purchased. These may include medication management, assistance with personal care, escort service to and from activities or events and nursing services. Assisted living residents can bring their own furniture and may maintain an automobile if they still drive.

Some assisted living facilities have specialized dementia units, and these range in size, configuration, staffing, training and resident selection. It behooves the prudent family member to ascertain exactly what makes the dementia unit a specialized unit.

Funding for assisted living is by self-payment more often than not, although some states will pay for some of it through their Medicaid programs. And some long-term-care insurance policies will cover this level of care. Assisted livings are generally more aesthetically pleasing than nursing homes, which is why families tend to prefer them. They also may be less expensive for individuals needing less care; however, the costs will increase with escalating care needs, all to be considered when making a selection.

SELECTING AN ASSISTED LIVING FACILITY

Assisted Living Facilities (ALFs) differ in facility design, atmosphere, size, sponsorship, staffing, services offered and costs. There are no national standards, and regulations vary from state to state. Availability also differs from area to area. If you think this type of care would be appropriate for your loved one, you need to select a facility that best suits his or her needs and preferences.

Gather as much information as possible: ask friends and neighbors, clergy, physicians and community leaders, and develop a list of possibilities. Then, do your footwork: arrange a visit, look around and ask questions—visit with or without your loved one at first, depending on his or her availability, cognitive status and stamina. If your elder is agreeable to your developing a short list to see at a later time, then do it. Then, you can both visit the selected facility or two, look at available rooms or suites and even try lunch. What should you look for?

The Facility

Is the appearance and design of the building attractive and pleasant? Is it clean, well-maintained and odor-free? Is it well-lit and cheerful? Are there attractive spaces for activities and dining? Is it easy to find one's way around? Is it user-friendly to people with mobility issues—Are there easily accessible elevators? Are showers handicapped-accessible? Are there wide corridors? Are there handrails in the corridors? Are all areas wheelchair accessible? What are the individual living units like? If there are licenses and inspection reports posted, look at them.

The Residents

Do residents look happy and comfortable, and do they socialize with each other? Are they engaged in various activities? Are they interacting with you as you are walking through? Do they appear to be appropriate housemates for your loved one?

The Staff

Are they warm and pleasant? Are they addressing residents by name and interacting with them? How many staff members are on each shift? What kind of training have they had? Who administers medications? How often is there a nurse in the building?

Services

Is there a written service or care plan for each resident? Who assesses their health and personal care needs, and how often? Under what conditions can a resident be discharged from the facility, and what is the procedure? What is the facility policy regarding storage of medicines, assistance with medicines and medicine record-keeping? Is self-administration of medicine allowed? If, in the future, a resident requires transfer to a nursing home, what are the facility's policies? Do they have arrangements with specific nursing homes? Some assisted livings are parts of larger systems of care or campuses that may include nursing homes and hospitals. It's important to get the facts.

Food Services

Are three nutritionally balanced meals provided every day? Are snacks available? Are special diets available—if so, what types? What is the dining room like? Who actually serves the food—wait staff or is this the responsibility of the personal care assistants? Under what circumstances can residents have meals delivered to their unit—is there an additional charge for this? Does the posted menu look inviting? Is a "satisfactory" kitchen inspection result posted?

Activities

Are the residents busy or just sitting around—glued to a television screen or snoozing? Do the posted activities look interesting and varied, and would they be interesting to your loved one?

Transportation

What are the policies for transporting residents to doctors' appointments, activities, shopping and church? What vehicles are used? Are they escorted to the appointments or just dropped off?

Dementia Units

Some facilities have specialized dementia units, and these vary considerably. As residents live in an ALF and "age in place," their cognitive abilities may decline, and they may require specialized services. Furthermore, families of individuals with dementia are turning to assisted living more and more because they are generally less costly and more attractive than nursing homes. Family members must ascertain exactly what makes the dementia unit special, including environmental features, staffing, staff training, food services, activities, what the typical resident looks and functions like and exactly what services are provided. Ask what the costs are and what extra charges are assessed. For example, some facilities assess an extra charge for incontinence care.

Contracts and Costs

Ask for a sample contract or resident agreement to review. You may want to run it past your attorney before you sign it. You also want to find out what happens when your relative runs out of funds—will the facility accept Medicaid, if it is available to your relative for this service.

SELECTING A NURSING HOME

Not all nursing homes are the same. Differing in size, ownership, services offered, cost and quality of care, each is distinct, to be evaluated on its own merits. Do not choose at random. Rather, some serious fact-finding is in order. However, be aware that in some areas of the country, the choices are limited. In a rural area, you may have only one facility in a fifty-mile radius.

A good shortcut to keep in mind is to develop a short list: Seek recommendations from your parents' physician, friends, clergy and neighbors. Call the local Office on Aging and a categorical disease association, such as the Alzheimer's Association, if this applies. Now that you have your select list, here are some pointers on what to look for.

Begin with the location. Accessibility and proximity have high priority, so you can visit easily. Traveling long distances will add to your stress level. Family members, like you, are a very important part of the care team. Even though you will turn over the day-to-day care to the nursing home staff, you will still remain a caregiver. However, your role will be somewhat different—information source, visitor, advocate, companion, soother and staff resource. Remember, what you provide to the new "care family" is most essential to your loved one's quality of care.

Find out what services are offered. Don't be afraid to ask. For example, if your mother has dementia, you might ask if there is a designated dementia unit and whether she's a candidate for it. If there is no special unit, you may need to address concerns such as whether there are measures in place to prevent her from wandering out of the facility unnoticed. You also want to know what special activities are available and whether staff members have received training regarding the special needs of individuals with dementia.

Conversely, if your mother is cognitively "sharp," what provisions are made for her? Is there a unit where special attention is paid to this type of resident, in terms of roommates, dining companions and activities? Or do these residents leave their unit for dining and activities? Look at the dining room during a mealtime. Look at the activities calendar. Attend an activity that you think might be suitable.

If your loved one requires rehabilitation, find out what that's all about— Exactly what services are offered? How many hours of therapies are provided each day? These usually consist of physical therapy, occupational therapy and speech therapy, in addition to the usual nursing home services. Some facilities also offer cognitive rehabilitation. Physical therapy entails working with balance and mobility, improving muscle and joint function, pain alleviation and teaching the use of assistive devices such as canes, wheelchairs and walkers. Occupational therapy offers improvement or relearning of Activities of Daily Living (ADL) and fine motor coordination. Speech therapy focuses on communication skills as well as swallowing abilities.

What you may also ask is does this facility have a special rehabilitation or "subacute" unit (names can vary in different places). A discrete unit suggests that there is a more homogeneous grouping of shorter-stay patients here. Some facilities are dedicated to rehabilitation exclusively and may be called rehabilitation hospitals or centers rather than nursing homes. And some nursing homes may have highly specialized rehabilitation units—cardiac or poststroke care. Note that the need for rehabilitation is often quite sudden, after a hospitalization for surgery or a stroke, and the choice of a facility needs to be quick and is dependent on availability.

Ask about the facility's financial policies. What are their charges as a private-pay patient? What is included in the rate? What happens if your parent's money runs out? Do they accept Medicaid? And will there be a smooth transition from private-pay status to Medicaid? Will they assist with preparation and filing of the Medicaid application? If they do not accept Medicaid patients (most nursing homes do), know this up front and consider other places if your parent's funds are likely to run out.

What about staff-to-resident ratio? It is logical that the fewer residents assigned to each Certified Nursing Assistant (CNA), the better the care. But, this is only the beginning of the story. First of all, there are three shifts of nursing assistants each day, and the numbers vary from shift to shift, usually with fewer on the night shift. In some instances, a smaller night staff may not be adequate. For example, sleep patterns change with dementia, and some individuals get their days and nights mixed up. When these persons are up at night, they need someone close by. Secondly, there are a variety of administrative and consultative nursing positions, including the director(s), the nurse-educator, the wound care expert, the infection control specialist and the Quality Assurance person. While these positions are all crucial, nonetheless, they are generally not of the hands-on variety. Actual nursing care is done by Registered Nurses and licensed practical nurses, who also assign and supervise the aides.

A very important indicator of the quality of nursing services is the continuity of care provided. This is measurable by the turnover rate among the staff and the proportion of temporary agency employees. The higher the rate of turnover and the use of agency personnel, the less likely it is that staff know their residents well and provide consistent care.

How about the environment? You went. You looked. You smelled. You listened. What was your first intuitive reaction? Did you feel like running, like crying, like screaming or like staying and learning more? Does the environment look attractive and well-maintained? Is the dining area clean? Are there unpleasant smells? Are there inviting nooks and crannies for conversation and privacy? Are there attractive areas and supplies for activities? Does the staff appear attentive and interactive with the residents? Do they seem to respond to requests promptly?

What's mealtime like? What does the dining area look like? How does the food look and smell? Are the residents served promptly? How helpful is the staff with unwrapping or uncovering food, opening milk cartons, using condiments and cutting food? Are there substitute selections available for residents who request them? Do the meals match the menu posted? Are there meals available that match your loved one's dietary preferences—vegetarian, kosher or culturally appropriate? Lunchtime is a good time to tour a facility, so that you can check these things out for yourself.

What are the activities? Look at the activities schedule that is posted. Does it contain variety and choices—entertainments, celebrations, small group activities, individual activities and religious services? Does it address special interests and needs? Are there evening and weekend activities? Are the activities areas attractive? Is the space sufficient for the number of persons using them? Are games, equipment and supplies readily available for individuals or small groups to do their own thing—start a card game, play checkers or chess, or use a computer? What about activities staff? How many are there? And what are their schedules—are they there evenings and weekends, at least sometimes?

And how about the quality of care? Information is available on the Internet through the nursing home report card, Nursing Home Compare or the Center for Medicare and Medicaid Services Quality Initiative. The report card provides information regarding the last survey by the state health department. Remember, this may have been a year or more ago, and things may not be the same—they may be far better if they were not so good then or vice versa. The quality initiative covers important factors such as pressure sores, development of infections, poor pain control, physical restraint use and loss in basic daily activities. As important as this information is, it is incomplete. Your senses will tell you a lot. Do the residents look well cared for and content?

Think about your loved one: all things considered, could she or he be at ease and well cared for in the facility, knowing what you know about her or him and also about the place. And think about yourself: putting your guilt and your ambivalence aside, do you feel you will be able to visit comfortably? If you've answered "yes" to these questions, trust your instincts and work with your parent and the staff to make it happen.

GETTING YOUR PARENT THERE

Says Russell, "I don't know how I'm going to get him there. I think it's great and just what he needs, but, oh, my God, getting him there . . . That's another story." This is a very common concern. While we will be providing a host of suggestions, some may not match your style. Adapt them, change them, but the important thing is to reach your goal—getting your parent placed.

While it's usually much easier going from the hospital to rehabilitation because it's medically ordered and a step closer to home from the hospital, this will vary. The best explanation you can give follows: "This is what the doctor ordered and will make you better. We'll be there to visit and will take you home when you're ready."

Going to an Assisted Living Facility or a nursing home for long-term care is a harder sell. If it's a move directly from the hospital, it's easier because there is an expectation of recovery. Moving an individual out of their home is fraught with minefields. Having been their cocoon for years, it's familiar. And now going from the familiar to the unknown is scary. No matter how much preparation there has been and how much insight they have, it's still fraught with danger in their minds. How does this affect you, the adult child? It heightens your already high stress level. But, don't get derailed. You need to be firm, goal-directed and empathic, all at the same time.

What if your parent has a dementia? How do you make the switch here? In many cases, you can't tell them much. And if you do, they don't remember it. Giving them advance notice doesn't help. In fact, too much talk can set off a catastrophic reaction. So what do you do? Basically, you have to just do. Whatever happens, you will handle it. Pack and load the car at night when they're asleep or when they're away from the house, to avoid or decrease agitation. On moving day, take a week's worth of clothing, their toiletries, family photos and a favorite afghan or object. If you can, get their things placed in their room at the facility before admission, so that it's a little familiar. You can bring the rest of their things at a less tumultuous time.

When you're ready to leave home, give them a favorite object to hold onto and maybe a favorite snack to have on the way. If they've been cared for at home by a home health aide, take that person with you to help get your parent settled in. Try to arrive at the facility in mid- to late morning, so that there is opportunity for the admission process with some distraction and opportunity for socialization. Your having lunch with them would be a great idea.

What do you actually tell them? Look for positives and capitalize on them. For example, if parents love music, emphasize the musical activities and the entertainments that they will be able to enjoy. If they have been social, emphasize the opportunity to be with other people. They may have been very isolated at home. If they have been falling, emphasize the fact that people are there for them and they are protected day and night. Be creative. Avoid taking hope away. If they keep insisting that they don't need to be there, you might respond with, "The doctor said you have to be here for now to help you to walk better or gain some weight or be with other people." Do not make any promises you can't or won't keep. Do not promise to take them home. Rather, use indefinites such as, "We'll see how you do." "Try it for a while." Assure them that you love them and will be there for them.

The first few hours—and possibly the first few weeks—are going to be rocky. With placement, elders face an identity crisis: "Who am I?" "What am I doing here?" They now have to adapt to someone else's procedures because no matter how "familylike" the facility is, certain basic routines have to be followed. Leaving their familiar surroundings represents a loss.

Your elder relative and you have a big adjustment to make. Know that you both will get through it. But also be aware that during this transitional time, you need to pay attention to yourself, too. To lessen your stress when you visit, bring someone with you for moral support—ask a friend, spouse, sibling, grown child or friend to go with you. If no one is available, visit during an activity that you can attend with your relative. And, in between your visits, try to resume your normal activities.

PLACEMENT: WHAT DOES IT REALLY DO?

With placement, we turn over the physical care of our loved ones to a facility and expect to feel a lot of relief. But this doesn't always happen. While the physical relief is there, the emotional consequences abound. After years of providing care, this placement is a loss, a loss of an all-consuming role and a job that structured our lives. Perhaps there's also a loss of face: You may see your action as a "failure" and imagine that others think the same. You may feel sad. You may feel bereft and mourn. And you may feel guilt. Intellectually, you will realize that you're guilty only of doing what had to be done. However, your emotional reactions will persist—especially the guilt. Said one son, "Even though I know that my mother is being very well cared for and is doing a lot better than before she went into the nursing home, I still have pangs of guilt every time I visit."

Even though you turned over the physical care, you are still anxious and worried about whether they've got it right. "What will they tell my mother when she calls out for me in the middle of the night? Will she be able to find the bathroom?" You really want to visit every day and hang around there. After all, you're the one who actually knows how to do it. Right? Generally speaking, the facility can and will take good care. With your help, they will become familiar with your loved one's habits, likes, dislikes and idiosyncrasies. These will be taken into account. If you can, visit regularly and encourage others to do so—neighbors, friends, other relatives and grandchildren—but do not hang around every day. After you get over your initial shock, realize that you now have some time and energy left for you. Now is the time to start rebuilding your life.

Sadie: A Successful Placement

Sadie lived with her daughter, Jenny, son-in-law, Eugene, and their family. As Sadie became frail and needed hands-on care, caregiving became an ever-increasing strain on Jenny's time and energy. Eugene felt that she was shortchanging him and the children. One day, Sadie fell and fractured her leg. Requiring surgery, she was hospitalized. The discharge planner urged the family to consider having Sadie go to an inpatient facility for rehabilitation. They all agreed. Sadie liked the facility and expressed interest in staying there long term. Recognizing how much had been associated with providing care for Sadie, Jenny and Eugene decided that placement would be good not only for Sadie but also for their marriage. For this family, placement was positive.

TIPS FOR SUCCESSFUL VISITING

Set realistic expectations: Your loved one may be more confused, disoriented or anxious during the initial adjustment period. Also, not everything will be perfect every time you visit. Your relative may have refused to go to the beauty parlor, even though you had specifically arranged an appointment. Her eyeglasses may have gotten mislaid. Try to problem solve as best you can.

Acknowledge your relative's feelings. Be empathic and open to the variety of responses that you will probably get with each visit; anger at you, anger at the food, anger at the staff, anger at the place and anger at life. Conversely, they may be happy with the food, happy with the nurses and still furious with you. Don't get taken over by the negativity. Also, do not become confrontational and don't try to rationalize it away. If your relative becomes nasty or volatile, cut the visit short. Calmly, tell them you need to leave now but plan to return soon. Feelings are feelings and let them be. That goes for you as well.

Optimize your visits. Plan visits to coincide with an activity you can share such as an entertainment or a party. Or, try to visit at a time of day when you can walk or wheel your loved one outside for a change of scenery and fresh air. Or bring an activity—a photo album, family videos, a pet, a grandchild, a news article, knitting, crocheting or sewing. After you become more familiar with the facility, you might visit together with another resident and their family member to make things more social for all of you.

Communicate with the staff. Get to know them. Learn their names. Thank them for their caring. Let them know the positives as well as the negatives.

We have laid out steps to make the transition to institutional life less painful for you and your older parent, but these steps are not always easy to follow. Human behavior has its own imperfections. Some children handle this process with total success, while others fail. In general, the well-intentioned child rides a seesaw between success and failure. Your most realistic goal in this major life change is to help your parent in the direction of a reasonably satisfying adjustment and, in the process, to achieve a reasonable state of mind for yourself. Patience, understanding and empathy will help you through.

The road to placement is full of potholes but most likely is a culmination of a long and torturous caregiving journey. For many people, placement signals irrevocable changes in familiar and valued relationships. But, be assured that you have done what needed to be done. Now, a team of caregivers will be taking care of your ailing elder. You are and always will be an important part of this caregiving team, but at least you are no longer doing a Herculean job alone.

9

When Your Parent
Is on the Difficult Side

$\mathcal{B}$elieve it or not, your parent was once a child, a teenager, an adult and is now an aging individual. She and her personality traveled the route together. While you didn't see the seed being planted and watch it bud, here is the tree, full grown. But underneath are tangled roots, also unknown and unseen to you. Difficult then means difficult now. Small cracks in the wall then may be chunks of empty space now. And you have to deal with it all.

What are the most difficult qualities to handle? Shakespeare's King Lear is an example: a parent who demands, not just asks for, continuous admiration and attention from his daughters. No longer able to command, his loss of self-esteem topples him into shame and rage at others. Needing constant applause, the hunger never ceases, and his daughters are rendered inadequate, no matter what they do.

What makes a parent difficult? It is the lack of awareness that he or she is difficult and the inability to acknowledge that his or her behaviors affect other people. Whatever their internal experience is, it spills over onto you, but they take no responsibility for it. As Oscar Wilde so judiciously observed, they look but do not see.

Did you always see them as difficult? No. As a child, all you really saw were two tall, magnificent giants, who took care of you, held you, fed you, nurtured you and, except in cases of abuse, were your hero and heroine. You idealized them, a normal part of development. They also mirrored you, understood who and what you were, and you flowered. But, now there is this change in their behaviors, not necessarily a part of aging.

Even in difficult people, behaviors vary. While we are not speaking of psychiatric diagnoses, when disturbing styles are frequent or intense, they can be problematic. Following are some behavioral characteristics that caregivers find most difficult to cope with.

THE MANIPULATOR

Manipulation is usually connected with con artists, who cheat, steal and use people to their own advantage, with little concern or care for others. Yet, manipulation, something we all do, can be of benefit. When someone tells you of a movie they would like to see and you immediately add, "Oh no, that got terrible reviews. Let's go to this other one. It got fabulous reviews—and I'm told it's a 'must see,'" you are manipulating. But, done with good intentions, it can have benefits, such as for the woman who got to see the movie she wanted to see.

Dan's father was another situation. "My dad wants to come live with me," says Dan.

> Is he kidding? Me take him in? He must be out of his mind. Do you know what kind of father he was? He was the manipulator of manipulators. It's a story for the books. He was married to my mom, and there were three of us, myself and two sisters, one older and one younger. As a detective, he was not home much. When mom asked him where he was, he always said he was "working on a case." Well, that's what detectives do—right? She was so sweet, so naive, but we loved her for these qualities. When she questioned why he sometimes took clothes with him or brought some home to be washed, he said that he often changed clothes in the car, to feel fresh again. There was always some excuse. And then one day, a friend of my mother's asked her if she was divorced. My mom said, "Oh, no we're not. Where did you hear that?" She said that she met someone at a meeting, who introduced herself as Mrs. ———, using my dad's name. That woman said that her husband was a detective and that they lived in an area close to my dad's work. My mother confronted my dad. And you've got to hear this one—yes, he had another wife—and two grown daughters with her. Of course, it's illegal, but he was a bigamist, and the three of us had two half-sisters. We were all in shock, confused, furious and demoralized. After Mom recovered from the shock, she divorced him, not forgiving and not forgetting. She managed to pull the pieces together and go on with her life. We watched in awe and stood behind her.
>
> My dad? He is now in a Veteran's Administration hospital, with some kind of disorder and ready to be discharged. And where does he want to go? To my home. Does he have any awareness of how he destroyed our family with his convincing lies and manipulations? No, none. Where should he go? He was able to manipulate before. Let him just keep doing it. They always manage, don't they? Just don't involve me.

What is your role in all of this? It is to be aware. The manipulator is not going to change. If you can feel for him or her, and it does not take too much out of you, where there is negative manipulation, as in the preceding story, do the best you can. Understand that this is a lifelong trait and just do what you need to protect yourself from becoming or staying a victim.

In this case, the hospital will arrange care for his father, and Dan knew that he would not be put out on the street. Too angry to take him into his home, there were others around who also felt the "slings and arrows." At a later date, Dan found out that the "other wife" did not want him, nor did her daughters.

HELPLESSNESS

In general, our society sees older people as infirm. Seldom do you see them playing tennis, running and winning a marathon, hear about them having an active sex life, or see them in a movie or on TV screens as lovers. And so, the rules of the game insist that older persons play it to the hilt: I am old, infirm, helpless, cannot do and cannot manage. You, my caring relative, must do it all for me. And not only that but also do it quickly and well and forget about yourself. And so, older persons sometimes use their infirmities to control—everyone. If they are living with a child, loud music cannot be played past a certain time, because "grandpa/grandma/mom/dad will be upset—they're sleeping, they don't like this kind of music or they feel dizzy," and so life comes to a near halt as everyone succumbs to the helplessness that puts them into the same mold: helpless.

A son is visiting his father in a nursing home. "She just won't do it for me," says the father. "Do what?" asks the son, knowing that his father is talking about the nursing assistant. "Well, she leaves me dirty." "What do you mean dirty?" The father is annoyed and says, "She won't wipe my behind." The son takes a long breath. "Why should she do that, Dad?" The father responds, "What's the matter with you? Can't you see that I can barely move my arms?" Hesitating, worried that he may overstep, the son says, "But, Dad, I just sat with you while you had dinner and saw you hold the fork, knife and spoon, take the food and put it in your mouth. Your hands seemed okay. You can do the same with keeping yourself clean." His father replies, "You just never understand."

The son did understand. Spelling out what the older "helpless" person is capable of will make you feel better, but won't accomplish much. You need to be aware and not get involved in this play. Stay with your effective reality testing, and hold on to your boundaries. If you want to test your reality, just double check with all those who take care of him. These problematic behaviors do not fly like Athena out of the forehead of Zeus, as in Greek mythology, but have been there long term, and will continue to be there. So will you, if you understand this.

THE HYPOCHONDRIAC

Some elders use their infirmities, real or imagined, to take charge. Every little ache or pain is loudly proclaimed as a major disaster that only happens to them. They're always preparing for the worst. When visited, they are likely to say to the person who is about to leave, "Let me say goodbye now because I won't be here tomorrow." And, as you may suspect, this may go on for years. Franny was one such person. From her late fifties on, she was constantly seeing the "dark angel" at the threshold of the door and was always "fixing to die." Constantly vocalizing her wishes, giving her prized possessions away and focusing on the futility of life, she "cried wolf" at every opportunity. When a real health emergency arose, medical intervention was delayed until too late, because no one believed her.

The hypochondriac has little insight into the workings of the body and its connection to the mind and the spirit. Totally scared, they see the body as a machine and expect perfection. Having little or no tolerance for fluctuations of the body or the connections to the influence of the mind, running to the doctor with myriad symptoms and complaints becomes a way of life—seeking reassurance that they will not die.

Disturbing to family caregivers, the constant "crises" stir up feelings of anxiety, empathy, fear and helplessness. How can they assess? And, asking the doctor once again makes them feel foolish. What should you do? First and foremost, in order to calm your care recipient, you need to stay calm yourself. Your relaxed energy will be soothing to them. Then, stay with your good sense of what's happening, and observe, observe, observe. Be detailed in your observations. If, in your viewpoint, the latest problem is out of the ordinary, err on the side of caution and take the necessary steps. The wolf is sometimes real.

SUSPICIOUSNESS

Basically, people who do not trust other people do not trust themselves. There is a range from mild suspiciousness, a personality trait, to extreme paranoia, a mental illness. The nontrusting person is cynical and has a negative view of life. Everyone is "out to get them." Things have a double meaning. Simple acts of kindness are misinterpreted: "You gave this to me as a gift, but what's the underlying reason?" Or, "You say you want to take care of me, but I know you're really after my money." Taken to the extreme, the paranoid person thinks their food or medication is being poisoned, government men are following them, television characters are watching them and, in severe cases, voices are telling them what to do, mostly for no good.

How do you handle this? Do not confront. That will just increase their suspiciousness, and you will become part of the system that they believe is hurting them. Instead, say something that will show them that you are there to protect them. This will lessen their vulnerability. Stay calm and offer reassurance. Comments like, "I understand what you feel"; "We'll see what we can do about it"; "I will taste your soup before you do" and "I'll make sure that never happens again" are helpful. The personality will not change, but the behaviors will be contained. Where overt paranoia threatens the safety of the affected person or others, there needs to be immediate professional intervention, such as an evaluation by a psychiatrist or a community mental health crisis team. A police escort may be needed to get the individual, involuntarily if needed, to a hospital Emergency Room. Often, paranoia can be controlled by medications. Hospitalization may be necessary.

If the suspiciousness is a lifelong personality trait, no doubt you know that by now. If, however, the paranoia is of recent onset, it requires medical evaluation and intervention. In the elderly individual, a sudden paranoia can have an underlying medical cause such as an unrecognized infection. Know that it's not your fault and there is help available.

OBNOXIOUSNESS

Do not take this as a psychiatric diagnosis. All of us have known obnoxious people and experienced their toxicity. Our normal reaction is to run. But, if it's a relative and you can't run, what then? Take it with three grains of salt and four of pepper and toss it all off. The person who is insulting to you really hates him- or herself. Examples might include the following: "Look at you. You're so ugly. Who would ever have you?" Or, "Look at the size of you. You're like a whale blown up." Or, "When losers were born, you were first on line." Know that these people basically are trying to project their huge disappointments in themselves onto you. It has nothing to do with you.

Set limits on the amount of time you spend with people of this nature, so that you don't become contaminated by their negative energy. Another strategy is to visit this person along with others, so you are not the only object of scorn or ridicule. In extreme cases, you may choose not to visit. Abuse is abuse. Another antidote would be to hire others, on a rotating basis, to do the caregiving. You, as one who has been there, can offer these paid caregivers your emotional support. Seek balance. Take some time to do things that give you joy, to reenergize you.

THE APPLAUSE-HUNGRY OLDER PERSON

Shakespeare's story of King Lear describes an aging parent, who suffers a precipitous loss of self-esteem when he can no longer command. Shakespeare sets the tone of the tragedy from the beginning: the king demands of his daughters that they profess their admiration for him precisely when he gives up the baton of command. This resistance-to-aging behavior occurs in persons for whom aging is experienced as a debilitating loss of self-worth, unless they can continue to be admired, acclaimed for who they are, what they possess and what they have accomplished. It is feeding a self that is depleted, with a hunger that is never satiated. When this type of person realizes they can no longer complete the project they have begun, fix the fixture that needs fixing or, for the male, perform sexually as he had in the past, the inner sense of failure leads to a feeling of shame. For them, becoming older is tragic. The applause is gone; the audience has decreased or disappeared. This is not the same as depression. It is a different type of sadness; the "fix" is to give back the applause, the attention, and reinstate what has been "snatched away" for no reason.

Marilyn: The Painter Turned Art Critic

Marilyn had been a painter of some note, having exhibited in smaller galleries and successfully sold her works at street fairs. Now, she could no longer do so, the arthritis in her fingers being so debilitating that she could not hold a brush. A loving mother, her four children were caring toward her and sensitive to her need for applause and appreciation. They came up with an idea. Said one of her sons to his siblings,

> You know what? My job lets me be my own boss. Mom is going to go down the tubes if we don't do something. Why not try this? She knows so much about art; few can match her. Why don't I contact the local newspaper? They have a column on art, and it was announced that their writer is leaving. I could take Mom to the galleries, and she could dictate her critiques, which I could print out from my laptop. I'm sure some, if not all, would be published and she'd be in the forefront again. Worth a try?

Siblings agreeing, the process began. Her name was now visible for all to see. She received acclaim and phone calls: "I loved your column. Your description of early Impressionism was terrific. I am astounded at all of your knowledge, and yet, you sound like such a young person." Her response to that was, "Well, I am young. If you're involved in life, you never grow old."

And so, to the person who needs the applause, give it. The person or persons requiring it are not mean, nasty or grabby; they are the hungry one, asking that they be seen and acknowledged for who they are and for what they can do. It's not always feasible to feed this hunger, but where possible, fulfillment will make life a smoother ride for all.

THE COMPLAINER

The complainer doesn't see the glass half empty. They see it as whole and full of imperfections. An exquisite observer, the complainer sees it all and is happy to share it with you, despite your feelings to the contrary.

Alice: Seeing the Glass Full of Imperfections

Alice is in a restaurant with her daughter-in-law. A well-known dining place, it was highly recommended and is her daughter-in-law's treat. The food has just arrived. Alice tastes it, looks up, and with a sharp upward movement of her head away from the plate, crooks her pointer finger toward the waiter and beckons: "This is ice cold. It must have been standing around for a long time. Also, it has absolutely no taste. Is your good chef off for the night?" Bending down slightly and showing no signs of impatience, he responds: "I'm sorry, madam. I can get you something else or I can have it reheated, whichever you prefer." "I prefer neither," she says, and waves him off.

How does her daughter-in-law handle it? Familiar with the behavior, she accepts it for what it is—does not analyze, correct or explain it to anyone else, all of which would be pointless. What she does is eat her food with joy, appreciate her surroundings and, most importantly, not take it in. Included in this is the choice, if she so wishes, not to dine with Alice too often.

For some people, staying with a complainer for any length of time at all does not work.

Stanley: Always Crying "Wolf"

Ian is visiting his father, Stanley, in a retirement community. Kissing his dad with a "Hi there, won't stay long" attitude, he sits down in a chair near him. "I can't eat. Something's wrong with my gums," says Stanley. Familiar with what's coming next, Ian replies: "Dad, there's a dentist here. I can schedule an appointment."

"A dentist? I don't know what school he went to, but he's not a good dentist."

"Do you want to see your old private dentist, Dad?"

"He is not much better," and then, leaning closer to his son, as though sharing a secret, Stanley says, "Don't you understand. No one, but no one cares about older people?" Staying quiet, Ian then tries to say something positive to redirect the conversation. "There's this movie the kids and I saw last night . . ."

Every option offered is dismissed and the person suggesting them demeaned and insulted. Ian, unable to tolerate this and feeling it as a throwback to his childhood, hurriedly tells his father that he has to go back to work and to call if he needs anything. Fervently hoping that he won't call, the son departs—to return a month later, groomed for what he knows will be another complaining session. The complainer may be the boy who cried "wolf" once too often, or conversely, there may be a real problem. You need to discern the difference and act accordingly.

THE CHAMELEON

With the chameleon, you never know where you're at. One moment, you're the idealized person and the very next, you're worthless.

Juanita: The Unpredictable Storm

"She's a chameleon," says the niece. "I hate to think of her as a lizard—who changes their color with what they're feeling—if lizards feel—but my Aunt Juanita certainly does both." Penelope laughs.

> One moment she is one way and, the next, a totally different person. No warning, it comes down—whoosh—and then it's gone—until the next time, and you never know when that will be. It reminds me of the time my husband and I were in an exotic foreign country. Our tour guide was explaining something about this magnificent statue. It was a cloudless day, white puffs over our heads, a blue-violet sky, and air like a warm bath you just stepped into when suddenly, without a warning or a drop or two to alert you, I was drenched in rain. Well, that's my aunt.
>
> She's my mom's sister and both my parents died in a plane crash, so you'd think I'd be close to her. But it doesn't happen. One moment it's, "You're such a wonderful niece. How lucky I am to have you. And, not having children of my own, though your uncle and I did try, having you makes up for it." But the next minute, it's the opposite—how I don't seem to care—never come to see her—she had this pain and I was not interested. And on and on. Her husband is very quiet, and now I understand why. Not knowing when the storm is coming, he just sits it out. Can't blame him, poor guy.

To deal with the chameleon, if the niece has the heart and the energy, she can try to be a soothing caregiver. Because the aunt did not have good enough mothering as a child, she does not have the resources for self-soothing, particularly in the later years when there is more stress. When faced with their inner terror of abandonment, the chameleon becomes overwhelmed by a sense of aloneness. Not recognizing that they had alienated others, they push away all that is positive so that, once again, they will not be disappointed or abandoned.

The caregiver needs to offer the "good-enough holding environment" that the aunt, in this case, never had. To do that, she has to have good enough feelings about herself in order to tolerate the intense fluctuations of mood, when the aunt seesaws from idealization, "You are wonderful" to, "You are a selfish, uncaring niece." Pointing out the contradictory behaviors to these persons does not help. They will either rationalize them or become angry or defensive and deny that any of this is true. The sad fact is that they need to feel in perfect control.

If your parent or relative has any of these qualities, and you, with a sense of self that does not easily fragment, can take it, it can also benefit you. When we reach out to another, no matter how difficult, it strengthens our own inner core. That is the payoff.

THE PENNY PINCHER

Penny pinchers are terrified that they will be impoverished at any moment. At that point, they will be cast to the wind, with no one to care for them. No one cares anyway. Making no or few connections with others, they are totally nontrusting and deeply feel that they have only themselves to rely on. They are both depleted and grandiose at the same time. If we peel away the layers of their childhood, there was no parent that was seen as a "god" in the home. Feeling unprotected and cynical, they believe strongly that there is no one to turn to. A self-fulfilling prophecy, this becomes a reality. Selfish and nongiving, they wear their armor tightly and live and die that way, having neither close friends nor family.

This person is not going to change. If you are a family member and the person is in need of care, your providing this would be a sign of empathic generosity and help to change your worldly outlook.

Henry: Stingy and Miserable

Henry, a twice-divorced man, is eighty-two and frail. Both his wives had divorced him. The second wife told his family, "He is miserable and stingy. He would have me spend hours looking for bargains on groceries, just to save a few pennies, when in truth, he had so much. Of course, I never got to know the exact amount. He would dole out money to me, as though I were a five-year-old asking to go to the candy store. And so I left." He had one daughter, Melissa, with his first wife. She had never been closely in touch with him, having left home at age eighteen, when her mother divorced him. Melissa witnessed the quarreling that went on at home and her mother being refused any kind of financial support. Henry did not spend money on himself either. After the divorce, he refused to support Melissa. She worked her way through college by waiting tables at night. Whenever she did speak to her father, he reminded her that "money does not grow on trees."

After Henry was hospitalized for severe congestive heart failure, Melissa was called when he was close to being discharged, the hospital social worker telling her that he was too frail to live alone. The social worker had questions about a suitable plan, since Henry told her that he had no money. If he had no money, he would need to provide documents for a Medicaid application. The social worker asked for Melissa's help.

Out of a sense of duty, rather than love, Melissa made herself available. Suspicious as her father was, but feeling his vulnerability, he reluctantly allowed her to go to his house. While he lived in a modest house in need of repair with few showings of wealth, she did find bankbooks and brokerage statements rolled up and hidden in his socks. He wasn't poor; in fact, he had a substantial amount of assets. Flooded with emotions, she felt a mixture of fury at him, pity for him and pity for herself at having been so needlessly deprived. When she went to visit him again, she blurted out what she was feeling, knowing, at the same time, it would not get her anywhere. She was right. He listened but explained that "you never know what might happen; you have to take care of yourself, and that's what I did."

Henry went home. His money needed to be used for his care. Because he had substantial assets, he was not eligible for Medicaid assistance, which has strict financial eligibility criteria. In order to get home care for Henry, Melissa would need access to his funds. Typically, he did not want to relinquish control. On the other hand, he was too weak to go to the bank and the brokerage office. And Melissa could not act on his behalf without legal authority, usually bestowed by a Durable Power of Attorney, which he had not granted. Finally, after much negotiation and energy expended by Melissa, Henry agreed to give her limited access to a single bank account. While far from ideal, this arrangement enabled her to get things going. As you may expect, there were many more hurdles to push through, but she was better prepared.

Penny pinchers are their own worst enemy: with their poverty mentality, they have a false sense of self that somehow cloaked them throughout life.

For example, there is the case of an eighty-nine-year-old woman with a net worth in the millions, who demanded that "low-cost" Meals on Wheels be delivered to her. She didn't like the meals and was constantly raging against the poor quality of the food and the lack of variety. Pointing out to her that she could afford anything she wanted was pointless. Her penurious image of herself was not to be challenged! And, like Henry, she prevented herself from getting amenities and services that would have enhanced her quality of life and enabled her to enjoy the money she had so diligently worked for and saved.

THE ALCOHOLIC

Late life alcoholism is on the rise, particularly after retirement and, most especially, for men. This is due to the fact that the loss of the work role is a stunning blow to their self-esteem and the structure of their lives. When asked, "What do you do for a living?" their being retired makes them feel embarrassed and inadequate. Some turn to alcohol for solace.

Wilbur: Double Losses

Seventy-two-year-old Wilbur had been an engineer working for an automobile company and recognized for his solid abilities. Retiring at sixty-five was attractive to him because of the lifelong benefits that were promised. Shortly afterward, his wife, Maggie, developed advanced breast cancer. Her illness was incapacitating, and he became the caregiver. Despite everybody's best efforts, she died within a year. While friends and family tried to offer comfort, he turned to the bottle. In the past, he had been only a social drinker, having a cocktail or two on occasion and not more than a glass of wine with dinner. The effect of the alcohol was to numb him, calm him, and help him sleep and forget the profound losses he had just gone through. While a partial "zombie," he felt better able to cope. Although he felt comfortable, others were distressed. Unkempt, untruthful and denying he was no longer the person his family and neighbors had known, he just insulted them and walked away when they tried to suggest treatment to him. One day, while crossing a street, he was hit by a car and taken to the hospital. While his injuries did not appear to be serious, they decided to keep him for observation. Not having access to the bottle and not admitting to being an alcoholic, he began to experience symptoms of withdrawal. Fortunately, these were recognized by the staff and promptly treated. Previously unaware of how overpowering his addiction was, family and neighbors were supportive of his receiving long-term treatment.

He eventually accepted the fact that he had to stay away from alcohol for the rest of his life.

Losses inflict great pain upon a person, and when there are multiple losses, the damage is compounded. Wilbur gave up his job and with it his lifelong identity as he perceived it. Maggie's death was a further stripping away of self. Now a widower, he had even lost his role as a caregiver. The bottle was all that he could depend on. And he did. Knowing this and having gained insight, he was now able to start rebuilding his life.

THE RAGER

When anger becomes a way of life, it has lost its basic function, which is to propel you into action. Like all emotions, in its normative state, it is a cueing mechanism. However, this was not so for Priscilla.

Priscilla: Angry at Everything

Seventy-year-old Priscilla was angry all the time at everybody and everything. Nothing was ever done right. No one was any good. The world was a jungle, in which only she knew how to survive. While she was healthy and independent, though she did not have close friends and no one wanted to hear her venom, she managed. She knew how to "charm" some people, such as her building superintendent, to get what she wanted. To the outside world, it appeared as though she managed quite well, until her ferocious independence was stripped away one day. Having had a mild stroke, she became confused and fell. She was found by the cleaning woman, who assumed she had been lying there for the whole night and called the paramedics.

Admitted to the local hospital, her fury was increased by her incapacity. While the hospital staff tried to help her, she pushed everyone away with her raging behavior—"Get away. Don't touch me. I'm fine. I don't need anything from anyone. You don't know what you're doing. I know my body." Though entitled to the good care that was available to her, she got very little of it, and only with great effort on the part of the staff. Her verbal abuse toward staff members and uncooperative behaviors led to the development of complications that might have been prevented.

Priscilla was never married and had no children but did have a devoted younger sister, who tried her best. She kept in touch by phone, but visited infrequently due to her sister's rageful, unpredictable outbursts. Unaware that Priscilla's cognitive abilities had declined, visiting her in the hospital was like "shock therapy" for the sister. Visits were cut short to the minimum. Despite her difficulty in facing her sister's current condition, she became the de facto primary caregiver and arranged for and supervised Priscilla's long-term care. In some circumstances, reluctant relatives change their behaviors and become interested caregivers against all odds.

THE HOARDER

The hoarder hoards. Nothing is ever thrown away. All can be used some-day—who knows when. The mess builds and builds until there's literally no walking space. Insects and roaches have to compete for space. The hoarder sees none of it, feels none of it and hears none of it. Any criticism from another person is blown off. Neighbors band together for eviction purposes and call police and fire departments but all to no avail. With the hoarding comes self neglect. While they may be hoarding things, the refrigerator can be empty or contain stale and moldy foods. Everything becomes a place for something to be stored. They often use the bathtub as a storage bin, while they remain unbathed. Unreachable, untouchable and estranged from family, no one knows whom to call in an emergency.

While they are strange and reclusive, they are not necessarily incom-petent. Somehow, they do manage to survive and hang in. The bane of the existence of social service agencies and government authorities, they stub-bornly do what they do, all attempts to the contrary. When, against their will, they enter the health-care system, discharge planning becomes the ultimate nightmare. What can be done? They won't allow anyone to clean their home, yet they will not leave it. And allowing them to go back means an "unsafe discharge." The courts may also be rendered helpless because they are often adjudged legally "competent."

This is a prime example of the tightrope that families and providers have to walk in gray areas. While these individuals do not meet the legal standard for incompetence, they are not functioning in reasonable ways. Even when they seem to present a danger to self and others, there may be no legal recourse.

THE OBSTRUCTIONIST SPOUSE

Dad is ill and needs care. Everyone knows it, you know it and try to help, but Mom says, "Thank you very much. He's fine, and I can handle it all." Such is the case of Jenny and Harold.

Jenny: I Can Handle It Myself

Jenny and Harold were married for forty years. Just after their fortieth anniversary Harold was diagnosed with dementia. Jenny decided then and there that she and only she knows what to do for him and how to take care of him. Their two daughters, who dearly loved their parents, wanted to help. Wanting to get the best care, they were willing to pitch in and help in any way possible. Constantly rejecting their offers, Jenny insisted, "I can handle it myself. He doesn't need home care or day care or assisted living—he's got me."

Harold had some other serious medical issues, including diabetes and ulcerative colitis. When these produced alarming symptoms, Jenny refused to take him to see a doctor or to allow his daughters to do so, claiming that "it's only his dementia getting worse." When, over Jenny's protestations, one daughter took her father to the Emergency Room with dehydration, Jenny protested that "the doctors were only trying to make a big bill—it's only his dementia."

Jenny was the spouse and also his designated Power of Attorney and Health-Care Proxy—his "everything." Carefully guarding her authority and refusing to share, her daughters felt helpless at the sidelines. However, in a crisis they all went to the physician or an Emergency Room together, demanding their mother allow him to get necessary treatment. Sometimes they got their way, but once the immediate crisis passed, Jenny would resume her dictatorial and obstructionist stance. Because Jenny was impossible rather than incompetent, the daughters could do little more than confront one crisis at a time.

There may be one family member who is the constant naysayer. What should you do? Take one step at a time, knowing that any time you get through is progress. Chinks in the armor are opportunities.

PUTTING IT ALL TOGETHER

Aging isn't always graceful. While some people step on other's feet, others trip on their own. Character traits, good and bad, have longevity and so, too, do associated behaviors. Some people are chronically difficult. Even though they may be your parents, they may also be problematic. And if you thought that this would wash away with old age, forget it. What was is and will likely continue to be. Thorny behaviors impact the care recipients, the caregivers and everyone around them. If the care recipient is hard to deal with, everyone shies away and the care is minimal. These behaviors heap an extra layer of stress on the sandwiched caregiver and provoke feelings of embarrassment, shame, guilt, disappointment, grief and anger, to mention but a few.

Do the best you can with the cards you've been dealt. An ace is an ace, but jokers are also in the deck. Your parent or relative of seventy, eighty or ninety years has deeply embedded traits. Despite your approval or disapproval, these have worked for them, since they have survived. The bottom line is to know who they are and work with them as they are. Equally important, and in no way to be discounted, is for you to know who you are and to accept your own strengths and limitations, so you can survive, too. Take charge.

Some character types will be easier for you to handle than others. Know this. For the traits that are impossible for you to deal with, seek other options. For example, get others to help, whether family members or paid caregivers, at home or in other settings. Honor your limits and establish strong boundaries for yourself. If you're on the way to burn-out, seek counseling or join a support group. It is essential to know, observe, learn and take action. And remember, in all of this, you are acting as a model for your own aging!

10

Emotions in Everyday Life

Life is a train of moods like a string of beads.

—Ralph Waldo Emerson

*M*ost people believe they know what emotions are. We think of emotions as special kinds of feelings and label them with such words as "happy, sad, angry and surprised." We live them as part of our daily life, expressing them in direct or subtle ways in our relations to friends, parents, lovers, coworkers and children. And they express their emotions to us.

EMOTIONS

Emotions are intrinsic to human beings. While we may conjecture about the emotional life of animals, for example, the pet looking sad or depressed at the death of their owner or caretaker, we are only conjecturing. To what extent they "feel," we do not know. But we do know about ourselves. That we have a range of emotions is indisputable; that they vary in intensity for each of us is also known.

If you are intensely emotional, you could experience anger as rage or fury. Conversely, if you are less intense, your form of anger would be described as annoyance or irritation. All of us are born with emotions but how we use them depends upon the situation we face. If someone dies, we cry. If someone attacks us, we feel fear and withdraw. If someone loves us, we feel a sense of closeness, safety and security. What all emotions have in common is the reason for their being: survival of the individual and survival of the species. Even when emotions are called negative, such as anger and fear, they cue us to act and keep us alive. Not to feel fearful when something is potentially dangerous leaves you vulnerable. On the other hand, feeling your heart being stirred with tenderness when somebody shows love toward you is a positive human response.

The list of emotions is wide. They are as follows: anger, anxiety, fright, guilt, shame, sadness, envy, jealousy, happiness, pride, relief, hope, love, gratitude and compassion. The following are some of those most familiar for caregivers with an aging parent or relative.

ANGER

Samantha was sitting there, sobbing. Dabbing at her eyes over and over again, crying was interspersed with quiet sighs. Barely able to speak, she whispered: "I don't know what came over me. I'm not like that. I can't even speak about it. It is too, too awful. How could I do such a thing? Who would believe it? I would rather die. That would be easier. I don't think even God will forgive me. I've prayed to Jesus and Mary, but will I be forgiven? I don't know." Calming down, she went on:

> I visited my mother at home. She is well taken care of by a live-in home health aide. Though I had just had a tough day at the office, I decided to pop in before I went home. John would be making dinner and putting the kids to bed, so I had a little time. He's a good man, you know. We started talking, the usual: how she was doing, any visitors, what she had for lunch. It had all been said many times before. I was on rote.
>
> And then it began: She asked me where I had bought my blouse. I told her. She nodded. Two minutes later, she asked me again, this time in a more agitated tone. I told her. A minute later, she repeated the same question. I just couldn't hold a decent conversation with her. Suddenly, I was a wild woman. Moving my chair closer to her wheelchair, I slapped her across the face. Thank God, I didn't injure her.

The sobbing intensified: "It was like there was a demon inside of me. I was dehumanized—so not me. How can I be forgiven? To say I feel guilty is the understatement of the century. I'm telling it to you, but I will never tell it to anyone else."

Samantha went "over the edge," unintentionally, but physically abused her mother. Though there was no obvious bruise and nobody saw her do it, abuse is abuse. Never to be done. Not ever to be condoned. Fortunately for Samantha, this incident preceded mandatory elder abuse reporting. Now, elder abuse is a crime with legal consequences.

What is the professional to do? As in many such cases, the professional has a two-pronged approach: One is to impart the correct information to the person she or he is working with regarding the consequences and to report as required. The second, longer term is to help the person make changes within themselves to prevent such future occurrences.

Anger as Linked to Aggression

Commonly linked to aggression, Samantha first felt anger. While aggression is considered to be the oldest impulse of all, the direct purpose of anger itself is not to enable us to escape threatening situations but rather to destroy or drive them away. An automatic reaction, whether young or old, it differs only in minor details, since any opposition from another person will automatically bring it out. Anger is an automatic reflex, like sneezing or coughing. While, for each of us, the intensity of our response is different, its intent is the same—survival. Despite this, expressions such as we see in the case of Samantha can be abusive, dangerous, destructive and even homicidal. Along with this our hearts contract with pain at the interaction between Samantha and her mother.

Dealing with Anger

In the past, anger was most often dealt with by punishment. But, it was soon recognized that this had undesirable effects. It didn't work. Another way was to segregate the person, while still another was to reward "good" behavior.

How could Samantha have handled her anger before it ran away with her? What can you do in a similar situation? Use your emotions constructively by expressing them, which can also be cathartic for you: "I am feeling so frustrated and angry. I am beside myself." No longer having the fury gnawing at her innards, Samantha can now reach for the controls. A powerful tool given to all human beings, emotional self-awareness is applicable in this situation and thousands more. If Samantha used this, she could also add, "Mama, I am truly upset. I just can't seem to get to you. You're not hearing me." The effect would be to gain recognition of her experience and express it within the boundaries of control.

Empathy and Sympathy

Samantha could make a giant leap into empathy. Empathy is like becoming one with the person. Different from sympathy, where you may "sit alongside the person and feel for them," here you "feel with them." You and they are one. Their experience is your experience. Whether or not you've actually had that type of experience is unimportant. For instance, someone, a friend, colleague or coworker, tells you of his or her army experience. You have never had such. Yet, you can honestly say that you have had similar ones: of terror, anxiety, suffering and so on. Concluding honestly that, no, you were not in a war like they were but did have similar feelings in other situations, you are being empathic. Samantha could have said this:

> Mama, I know and feel how hard it must be for you to ask the same questions over and over again, not knowing how to get past that and not understanding what I am trying to say. How frustrating it must be for you to think of words, grasp for them and not be able to gain hold—and, deep down to know that this is not like you used to be. How exasperating. It would make anyone feel awful. I feel for you and do what I can to help. Know that I say it with all my heart.

Here, Samantha is sharing her empathic understanding and offering cooperation, care and love.

If following the above, Samantha has made three important changes: Changing the focus of attention, she has moved it away from the violence within. She has reinterpreted the situation she finds herself in. Her response now modified, it can be extended to similar situations.

As with all emotions, anger is not necessarily a one-plate meal. It may come in a combination of feelings, some more dominant than others, some equal and not readily identifiable. While Cornelia used the hospitalization of her husband, Woody, as a platform to express her pent-up anger, it was lifelong for Woody.

Cornelia: The Angry Wife

Woody was twenty-two when he was drafted into World War II. Healthy, big and strong, he came from a small western city and was planning to marry his childhood sweetheart, Cornelia. War changed it all. He saw the worst: lived in the jungles of the Pacific, had malaria, was covered with mud and gook much of the time and, as a machine gunner, shot on sight whatever moved. He said, "I didn't question. It was not anger—it was survival. It moved. I shot, no matter. I had to stay alive." And he did.

Coming home, he resumed his life. Opening a small business, Cornelia sometimes helped him out, but the marriage was often a shouting match; he, short tempered and "impossible to be with for too long, I just wanted to run but hung in."

At age seventy-six, Woody had a stroke and was sent to a Veterans' Administration hospital for treatment. Now ready for discharge, Cornelia was called: "We have good news for you. Woody can come home." After a long silence, finally, a voice came through: "He may be discharged—but not to me. He can't come back to this home. I've had enough of his abuse. It's your turn now." The phone clicked off. Hearing about this, Woody was furious, using words reserved only for Army buddies. He raged and raged, but few listened.

Caught in this crossfire was Doreen, their daughter. Now in her mid-forties, she had left home for an out-of-town college and married young. She pleaded with her mother:

> Mom, I know how hard it must have been to live with Dad all these years. I saw it. His temper was always on the edge. His language at you was what most women would not tolerate. And I could feel that if you had responded with your own feelings, it would have only made matters worse. So, you had to keep things inside to survive. I watched with horror and felt so helpless. I loved both of you. But, I hated his behavior towards you. Caught in it all, I couldn't wait to leave home. Thank God, that out-of-town college took me. And then I met my husband, who is the opposite of Dad. Our marriage is heavenly. Mom, please hear me out, Dad is now an old man, and I can't help but feel for him. He is my father, after all. And truth is, he went through hell in the war. Now he has no place to come home to. Could you find it in your heart to let him come back?

Pleading was futile.

Visiting her dad a short time later, Doreen sobbed and sobbed: "I don't know what to do, Daddy. You know you can come to live with me, and the girls can share a bedroom." Woody refused: "No, honey, I'd just be in the way. I can go into a V.A. nursing home, and they'll take care of me." Crying and hugging, he said, "I'll be okay there. It's a good place, and you and the girls can visit me. Really, it's okay. Not to worry." And Woody went ahead with his plans.

Cornelia called him occasionally on his private phone, which Doreen had ordered for him, but said that seeing him was "just too much—too many bags full of old angers that she wished not to stir up again."

Anger as Blame

And so, anger reared its head and stayed embedded, encrusted, to be displayed and acted on when, as Cornelia experienced it, the appropriate time came. Call it an awakened conflict between two persons, where you feel you have been affronted in some way. It was there and we, as humans, have a long history of conflict. Anger and possibly aggression generate an impulse to retaliate, but not all people do. What is the answer? Be aware and take another path. Change, as we have seen, is always a human possibility.

Anger doesn't have to be long standing. It can—and frequently does—crop up with illness or disability. Often, it generates blame, sometimes directed at another person and sometimes directed at oneself. "If I had not gone out in the rain and slipped and fell, I wouldn't be where I am now." "If we hadn't eaten in that awful restaurant you were so crazy about, I wouldn't have this parasite and be suffering now." It can also be displaced, as, for example, when a person is in a hospital or nursing home and faults the food, the room, the heat or lack of heat, the staff—everything. In some cases, the anger is vented at the caregiver, who becomes angry at the care recipient because being blamed for everything despite giving their "all" renders them feeling unappreciated, helpless, used and thrown away.

AGGRESSION

Aggression, while similar to anger, is not quite the same. While anger, the emotion almost everyone feels at one time or another, generates the impulse to attack, we don't always act on it. Anticipating the possibility of retaliation, we control ourselves. Aggression is different, its intent being to do harm to others. This intention is recognized by the legal system, which holds that an accidental injury or death is a lesser crime than a deliberate aggressive injury or death. Being angry is an early step in the aggressive mode, an indicator that the aggressive impulse has been aroused, which may, at times, result in violent behavior.

GUILT

Samantha, by striking her mother, had violated a moral imperative. Guilt was the result. Beginning with early childhood, the infant and child needing, wanting and getting love, the cloud of losing that love hanging over us, we descend into self-punishment. That is guilt. The direct connection between guilt, atonement and forgiveness includes forgiving yourself through a form of repentance. Where this connection is consciously made, peace can be yours. When not, guilt stays there, like a viral infection.

For some caregivers, guilt may come from feelings of "not doing enough." But, being only human, you need to set limits. Sometimes, a situation calls for seemingly harsh decision-making. In reality, it may be the only recourse that makes sense. A woman in her eighties, with a host of disabilities, refused help of any kind. It was only when her daughter had not heard from her, and repeated phone calls were not returned, that she went to check things out. Having her own key, she found her mother on the floor—she had been lying there for two days, unfed, dehydrated, incontinent and in pain, having fallen during the night. It was then that she forcefully insisted upon placement, even though her mother had consistently, and with great feeling, reminded her, "Don't put me away. I'd rather be dead." This daughter was "guilty" of caring.

Some emotions are not, as is anger, communicated through the use of words. Guilt is one of these. While we may think we see the emotion in the person, as in guilt, it may not be so. Blushing, you may feel, is a sign of guilt. But, equally, it can be an expression of shyness, some skin disorder or covering feelings of shame. While guilt does not necessarily lead to a more adaptive way of functioning, changing your ways for better ones, it can lead you to a reassessment of what moral code you broke and what you want to do about it. By moving the guilt into some other, more positive emotion, you have made the switch, and a good one. For guilt comes about in your sense of being accountable for violating your internal standards—those in which you believe and by which you live. As with all emotions, they exist for us to be motivated and as organizers of our behaviors. In effect, they are messengers, sometimes fierce, sometimes gentle, but messengers nonetheless. But, as with all messengers, we need to be there to open the door, listen and follow their advice. The daughter who found her elderly mother on the floor worked not on her guilt, but moved her working guilt into a form of help. She did something to keep her mother alive. So, guilt can be a quick change agent, or you can stand mired in it forever. As with all decisions, the choice is yours. This daughter made the only one that made sense. We all have that option.

SHAME

While guilt is generated whenever a boundary, set up by our conscience, is crossed, shame takes place when a goal that we set for ourselves as an ideal is not being reached. Flooding our whole being, it is experienced as deep, deep pain—failure. When shame is aroused, the underlying fears are those of ridicule, scorn, criticism or abandonment. Fiercely painful, what we do when we feel shame is to withdraw, thus limiting self-exposure.

Martin: Long-Standing Shame

Martin had always felt shamed by his father, Tomas. A wealthy man, Tomas had shown little affection to his wife, son and daughter. An entertainer, his time was spent accumulating mistresses. He used his young son as the "doer" or the "getter." "Go to the store and get this for me," Tomas would demand. "And do not come back until you have it." Martin always obliged.

When clothes needed to be bought, Martin outfitted himself in designer everything, but his son was taken to a thrift shop. Despite it all, Martin decided on a career in law. When time came to appear for his first job interview, he asked his dad to buy him a new suit. Again, he was taken to a thrift shop. He said, "I looked and felt like a scarecrow—the pants were way too long, so were the sleeves. I looked cheap, felt shoddy and was embarrassed and ashamed. Everyone else was dressed appropriately. And there I was, the outsider. All that money. What good did it do me?"

When Tomas was placed in an Assisted Living Facility, Martin seldom visited. When he did, his father gloried in stories of the old days, particularly of his gorgeous mistresses. Language sexually explicit, he said, "Well, you see, son, that's what it's all about. I had this babe up in my room and I . . . that's what women want. You are an OK kid, but weak—real men know what to do with a woman." And he would laugh.

Consumed with feelings of shame and fury curdling inside of him, Martin never let it spill over. As a lawyer, he had learned self-control. Choosing to work with the disadvantaged, he was much appreciated for being very compassionate. Strong feelings of outrage at anyone being taken advantage of won him many cases. In an excellent marriage, he had found someone who truly appreciated him and helped soothe earlier childhood experiences. Never wanting to repeat being the kind of father his dad was, he was a loving parent, becoming coach to his two sons' sports teams and a caring, available parent to his three daughters.

Visiting Tomas as infrequently as he could, he stayed just long enough to deliver some asked-for things and could not wait to leave. When Tomas died and Martin was called, he came—late. Tomas had asked to be cremated, and have his ashes thrown into the ocean, not far from where he lived. At the service, someone else gave the eulogy. Staying true to himself, Martin came late and kept quiet. When asked why he was late, he said that he had to appear in court and "traffic was terrible getting here." Deep within himself, he knew, for the first time, that he was now free. While Martin's shame was long-standing, all who knew his situation were amazed that he survived so well.

Shame can be short lived, temporary or illness related, but just as devastating. Caregivers, in particular, need to be conscious of the state of embarrassment or shame that their care recipient is causing them. For example, the parent who now speaks in expletives: f——, f——, f——, or the one who is sexually inappropriate. They also need to be aware that their parent, too, may now also be ashamed of their newly acquired, unasked-for body image: the woman who has scars on her face from surgical removal of cancerous growths and doesn't want to look in the mirror; the man who has had his face disfigured by Parkinson's disease or a stroke and may not want to have visitors; or the woman who has had an amputation and is afraid for her grandchildren to see the affected leg. While these altered body images cause their owners shame, they are not to be denied. Rather, they are to be dealt with as the painful realities they are, with compassion, empathy, acceptance and love.

ANXIETY

Says Josef, "I think I was born anxious. The cry that kids do at birth was not just a cry of coming into this world. For me, it was one of anxiety." He attributed it all to his mother, Teresa.

Anxious Son

Teresa was born in Poland and lived through the war—or, as she says, "If you can call it living." But, she survived and came to the United States as a young woman. Meeting a Russian man who also had emigrated, they married and produced Josef. As she tells it, Josef was her "beautiful boy," though she dressed him more like a girl. Going to school he felt strange, but she kept reassuring him that he need not look like the others because he was so special.

Considering herself a doting mother, unaware that she saw her son as an extension of herself, Teresa constantly threatened to leave him if he did not comply with her every demand. Powerless, he did. In his beginning teens, Vladimir, his father, disappeared. Left alone with his mother, anxiety became his everyday mode, its dimensions of uncertainty and fear of danger always about to emerge.

When Josef was in his mid-teens, Teresa married a very wealthy and, as Josef experienced him, a "sweet, sweet man," Wyatt, who adored Josef as a son. In turn, Josef clung to him, until the day he died. Josef was now a newly married young adult. Overcome with grief, he mourned deeply, clinging to Sherry, his new wife, who was nurturing, accepting and a replacement for the father he had lost. He, in turn, clung to her, too. While money had never been an issue, now, for the first time, he experienced the joy of using it. It was a world he had never known.

Describing Teresa, he said, "It made me dizzy. One moment, my mother was the benevolent queen, the next, without any warning, she became Cinderella's stepmother. And I never knew what to expect." Some years later, Teresa, now suffering from a host of chronic ailments, was placed into a luxurious nursing home. Said Josef, "I hate to say it, but finally I am free. My jail did have an escape hatch, after all."

Despite the anguish he had gone through most of his life, he does visit Teresa every day: his choice. "She is my mother. She can't help being who she is, the war and all that. And I guess, in a sense, there's a reason for it all."

There is a purpose for all emotions. Sometimes that is clear, but what is often unclear is that learning can take place, despite the so-called negativity of the emotion. Anxiety is one such. Having been explained as a disorder wherein we detect, focus on, store, retrieve and recall anxiety-related information, we can cut through that sequence by not doing the retrieving. By doing this, we limit the response, changing the automatic series of responses so that the warning that danger is coming, the retrieving, is changed to something that offers hope instead. In other words, we have cut through the wiring and substituted something more beneficial. This is what Josef did.

GRIEF AND MOURNING

Grief occurs not only with death but also with other losses such as retirement, declines in health and placement of a loved one in an Assisted Living Facility or a nursing home. We mourn for others as well as ourselves. Retirement can arouse grieving.

Involving multiple losses—loss of a job, loss of income, loss of a role, loss of a daily routine and loss of status, retirees experience sadness, grief and, sometimes, depression. On the other hand, for some retirees, there is relief rather than grief and a welcome entry into a new phase of life.

Yet, for some, declines in health and ability to function may include becoming unable to walk, to see, to hear or to reason. Having to rely on others for help with even the simplest or most personal activities, we may experience loss of independence and dignity—and grief.

Placement of a loved one in a facility for long-term care is a difficult, grief-producing experience. For some, it represents losing a piece of your own self in the bond, the attachment, you had for another. Death is the ultimate loss.

Clara: Still Grieving for Her Mother

"I walk into the house and automatically reach for the phone," says Clara.

> My mom has passed on more than a year ago, and I still can't believe it. Isn't that silly for a sixty-year-old woman? I used to call her each day and smile to myself when I heard her voice and the usual answer to my question of, "Mom, its Clara. How are you doing today?" She would say, so

softly, so gently, "Like an old woman, darling. How else can I be?" Familiar words, I couldn't hear enough of them—and now they're gone—with her.

Clara loved her mother deeply. It was a bond that went back to childhood—her mother, widowed at an early age, the protector, the caregiver, the nurturer, the "all" to Clara, the child, the adolescent and the adult. And now, Clara was feeling the loss of this very special bond.

As with all emotions, there is a range—grief begins with sadness, feeling blue. It may be relatively short in duration or may result in depression, a serious clinical condition that can be long-lasting. As humans, we grieve.

Grief is both anticipatory to and the aftermath of loss. Like the flame that glows softly or blazes, it is always there, to be ignited by the hint of a loss-to-be or one that just happened. In either case, it is felt as an identity ripped off, a piece of you no longer existing, the attachment you had to another you cared about and loved deeply. Just the thought of its happening, "She is very ill, and we don't know if she will survive," makes us feel naked, defenseless and totally vulnerable.

And then, the loss. Now it is real, and you feel as though you have crossed the river, the divide between the living and the dead. While the pain is intense, it can be felt deeply as a wound that may never heal. Your face to the world takes different forms. You may seem cool, accepting or brave—or, in contrast, hysterical, out of control or off-center. In truth, during these times, we are out of balance, plunged into an abyss of distress, which leaves us unstrung, sleepless and empty.

Yet, grieving, mourning and the human capacity to be are allowed, as others come along to help put meaning into it all. The rites, to make sense of what seems meaningless, include remembrances: "Mary was such a wonderful person. I remember when . . ." "John, when I first met him, was . . ." They put a face on that which is faceless, the void, the pit. It now has substance. And those of faith may comment, "He is now with God, home at last. It awaits us all."

Soon, the immediate shock, the grief, moves into mourning, like the heavy rains into a light but unyielding drizzle, to be dredged up at any moment throughout life: a person who looks like them, a movie, a memory or a dream. Suddenly, the flashback is there. Grief and loss—and death—all are there to bring us closer to ourselves. That is the meaning beyond meaning that bears the stamp of truth.

In addition to negative emotions, there are positive emotions. Love and hope are two of the positive emotions. These emotions have been called "restorer emotions" because they facilitate coping processes and are reenergizers.

LOVE

Love, meaning attachment, can be different for different people. While it is usually thought of as only romantic intimacy, it is more than that, being a bond between two people. You, the caregiver, may not think "love" as regards the care recipient, but nonetheless, you have formed a bond, one of the primary properties of love. Your care recipient is in the same position: they may or may not feel love for you, but they also have formed a bond. Chances are when you are apart, you miss each other.

HOPE

Hope, similar to love, is also a restorer and reenergizer. Hope is the belief that things will work out no matter what. For example, the cancer patient who can do little to curb the progress of the disease can still feel hope through faith in the doctor, God, luck and so forth. The hopers are generally the optimists, the ones who see the glass half full all the time. Even if you, the caregiver, are not particularly optimistic about the care recipient's condition, know that your care recipient's having hope can contribute to the healing process. Don't underestimate this.

• 11 •

Caring for You, the Caregiver

Everyone is focused on my parents, but what about me? When is there going to be time for me. Doesn't anybody care?

—A caregiver

It's not only your care recipient who's aging; it's you, too—every day. Your vision of yourself as a caregiver is a piece of the vision you have of yourself as a unique human being. It is perhaps an unexpected piece but there, nonetheless. Now that you have been thrust into this role, do not neglect your essential self.

Caring for one's aging relatives can be a round-the-clock job. It can be labor intensive and emotionally exhausting. A sleight of hand, the caregiver must juggle multiple roles: parent, child, caregiver, employee, employer, spouse and repairperson, to name but a few. Compounding this are time management issues. Burn-out can loom large when it seems that everything is falling apart all at once.

To prevent burn-out while devoting yourself to the challenges, stresses and rewards of this task, paying attention to your own needs is critical. This means to focus on your very human vulnerabilities, limitations and priorities. Your own health concerns and care are not to be ignored—especially at this time of heightened stress. Otherwise, you will be the second patient in the mix.

Caring is two-pronged: there is caring for the other and caring for the self. Both are part of the human experience, and both are essential. The key is to keep them in balance. For the caregiver, being kind is vital. Not less so is using restraint, setting boundaries. The person caring for an older relative who overdoes is one who is burning the toast.

135

Irene: The Care-Giver

Gus was a retired foreman of an auto assembly plant. Married for forty years, his devoted wife, Irene, was a homemaker, always attentive and attending to every detail, day and night. Though he was perfectly capable of taking a snack by himself, he would wait for her to anticipate his need and hand it to him, getting ruffled if she did not do so. She never protested. Soon after retirement, Gus began to have shortness of breath, which was diagnosed as congestive heart failure. Given medication and advised to simplify his routine and avoid overactivity, Gus took to his easy chair and stayed and stayed and stayed. Irene became his devoted caregiver, nursemaid, housekeeper, entertainer and all-around utility person.

He was relentless, and she set no boundaries. Neglecting her own needs, she ignored several episodes of her digestive problems, not discussing it with friends or seeking professional advice, convincing herself that his needs were primary. Tuning in to Irene's constant caring for Gus, her friends stopped visiting and calling. Finally, if reluctantly, she did hire a part-time health aide to assist. One night, her gastric distress became so acute that she was rushed to the hospital and found to have an advanced cancer and a short life expectancy. Immediately, the adult children, whom she had shut out of their father's care, insisted that she employ a full-time aide, now for the two of them. Three months later, after Irene died, Gus started to call the aide "Irene."

As with Irene, having no boundaries keeps you unaware of what's going on with your self. To know when we overdo and overspill, we must know ourselves. What appears to you as circumstances, conditions and even material objects are really the products of your own consciousness. You and your environment are not separate; in fact, you and your world are one. Instead of looking only at the "objective" appearance of things, look to the subjective center—your own self, your consciousness. Your reactions to what is reveal where you live subjectively, and this, in turn, determines how you live in the outer, visible world. You must be aware of being healthy if you are to know what health is. To know what relationships are all about, you must be aware of other people.

NARCISSISM

The word "narcissism" has been given a bad rap, always seen as something wrong, a focus on the self committed by a selfish, self-absorbed person. "She cares not for anything—or anyone. Her focus is only on what she needs, not caring about anyone else." If this is true for the person in the younger years, it will likely be true for them in the older years. "My mother only cared about how good she looked," says Harriet. "If I bought something new, she never complimented me on it. Instead, she would say, 'Oh Harriet, that would look great on me in blue. Can you get me one in my size?' So self-involved—and she never changed." Yet, Harriet, desperately seeking her mother's love and approval, always gave, seeing her two or three times a day, the underlying need never to be fulfilled.

SELF-CARE

Says one caregiver, "I need to nurture, feed, value and honor myself. That's what self-care is, remembering that I have a self. Then I'm alive. I'm well. Then I can help another person." Self-care is very different from narcissism, selfishness, self-absorption or self-indulgence. We require both physical and psychological nourishment and sufficient rest to restore our well-being in order to give to others and ourselves. Healthy narcissism, for example, can be seen in the older woman who, recovering from a stroke, asks for a comb and some lipstick, saying, "I want to comb my hair and look good. And, please, can you help me on with my earrings—you know, my favorite ones—in the drawer right near my bed?" That is healthy, to nurture and value yourself and remember that you are alive.

THE SELF

The self is your unique constellation of traits that make you who you are. You use these to interact with your environment in your own particular way. When you encounter new information, you will only take in that which is congruent with your character. This unique "you" flowers and grows. All of this combined gives you a sense of wholeness and integration, which you use to meet challenges and cope with the world. By-products of this are self-regulation and self-control, a balance. Self-regulatory abilities are critical for impulse control, essential to the development and maintenance of healthy self-esteem.

OUR MANY SELVES

We have a "true" self and a potential "false" self. The former is your unique combination of feelings, abilities, preferences, affinities and tastes. Your "false" self is one that forgoes your true self, being overly compliant as a result of trying to fit in. This fitting in has to do with the public self that we present to outsiders as a way of winning favor, to heal psychic wounds. Examples include the child who is shown off to others as "my darling, my gifted pianist" but was made little of at home, where there was no audience; or the young man whose mother did not cut his curls until he was four, showing off to others "my beautiful boy," while she dressed him as a girl, to his humiliation.

DREAMS

How do you get to know your true self? You find your self by getting to know your own needs, wants, preferences and abilities and staying close to your intuitive feelings. Your intuition is your first voice and generally the one that you can rely on the most. You also get to know this by using your dreams, both waking dream states and night dreams, as information about your true self. Your dreams are the concretization of what is going on in your life day by day. Easy to read once you take the time to feel them through, it is your true self talking to you.

It has been acknowledged that everyone dreams. You may not remember your dream. To counteract this, as soon as you wake and know that you have had a dream, write it down. You do not necessarily need a professional to interpret your dream, nor do you have to know symbols. Take the dream for what it is: you at this moment in your life. As for symbols, Freud said, "A cigar is sometimes just a cigar."

Tess: Nothing Could Stop Her

Tess, seventy-four, was a care recipient who had knee replacement surgery, rendering her temporarily immobile. Previously she had been an active person, who jogged, rode bikes, went hiking and prided herself on being young for her age, saying, "I can keep up with anyone at any age." And she could. After her surgery, it was another story. Outwardly, she was not depressed, nor did she experience this inwardly. Her continuous dream during this period showed how she coped:

> I woke up every morning exhausted, having been running to catch a plane that I always missed. Somehow, I couldn't run fast enough, or they just didn't wait for me. Then I realized that I could take the bus and get there just as well. It might take a little longer, but I would get there just as well, and the scenery was beautiful. I had been told so. When I learned how to

use this dream, I realized that the knee replacement had slowed me down but that somehow I would get around to doing what I needed to do and going where I needed to go. It might take me a little longer, but darn it, I would get there. Nobody and nothing could stop me. And the surgery was certainly not going to get me down. I still had years to live—and live well.

Tess's dream revealed her nature and the way in which she handles things in everyday life. Reflecting on it, she knew that things would be alright.

On the other hand, Calvin saw the clouds, and his dream was onerous.

Overcoming Terror

Calvin, seventy-nine, was a retired junior high school gym teacher, doing some freelance sports officiating in his retirement. Having had several bouts of persistent hip pain, he was told that he needed a hip replaced, the sooner, the better. However, he had never been hospitalized in his life and wasn't going to break his record now. In fact, he was terrified. As he told it to his best friend, who had been a school colleague,

> I wake up with this nightmare. I am lying in a sarcophagus like you see in the museums, all wrapped up in bandages like a mummy. I touch myself and know that there is no opening, and as much as I pull at the bandages, I can't get any of them off. But somehow I know from the feel and the size of it that it is a sarcophagus, and I am sure to die there. At that moment, I wake up, sweating profusely, breathing hard and, while happy to be alive, terrified that I can't seem to shake off this dream.

Once he could look at this dream, Calvin understood that it was his fear that surgery would render him totally incapacitated, helpless and trapped. Discussing it with his friend, who had hip surgery, he was reassured and gathered the courage to do what he had to do. Things went well, and the dream never recurred.

JOURNAL ENTRIES

One way of becoming more aware of who you are, particularly in the role you now have as a caregiver, is to keep a journal. We usually think of this as something that kids or adolescents do. But it is a very helpful process for learning about yourself at any age. It need not be lengthy. Just put down a paragraph or two, each day, as to what your day was like. Make it an abstract—or a trend of your feelings, your thoughts, your desires, your needs and your wishes. Read it at the end of each month, and see the track you're on. Note the pattern. It will reveal your path: a surprise, a delight or a new insight. You are right there.

INNER PEACE

How can you become and stay relaxed and in balance? Stillness is one approach. Take some time out for this. We think and overthink; we analyze, speculate, plan, reflect, calculate and obsess, going from subject to subject. While the mind is a miracle in itself, it also needs to be stilled. Only in moments of silence and total solitude do we discover that this miracle, our mind, is out of control. Speeding aimlessly on its own track, it breeds anxiety within us. We may become aware of this in our breathing, which becomes heavy and erratic.

Entering the heart of stillness and discovering true inner peace needs to be a focus for caregivers. Indeed, tasting the sweetness of this inner silence makes you more profoundly aware than ever before. It leads to that state of being called self-observation and, for some, "enlightenment." This is the state of all-encompassing peace—a sense of being "at one" with the universe, or simply "letting go."

So, in your busy, overactive, often frenetic days or nights, take some time out for stillness. Go into any room that has quiet you can depend on. Close your eyes and stay absolutely still. When thoughts invade you, see them as a flock of birds above you, flying off to some other land, and now, the air is clear again. Only the quiet and you exist. Do this each day, preferably at the same time, for a few minutes. No equipment, only your desire to be free and balanced is needed. And peace is yours. As this practice becomes more integrated in our lives, periods of tranquility become more penetrating. They evolve from momentary and transient experiences to familiar companions.

Once you have learned how to still yourself, you may want to go on. Yoga may help, prayer works and also meditation. To do yoga, you need a teacher, so join a class and begin. For prayer you know what to do. For meditation, here are some original exercises we have found to be most helpful: simple and easy, they can be done by you.

MEDITATION

Choose a quiet place for your meditation, and try to stay with this same place and same time of the day or night, if possible. In the beginning, five to fifteen minutes is enough, as long as it is consistent. Start by relaxing each part of your body and then take in a deep breath, slowly, and exhale through your mouth, quickly. Repeat three or four times. Now you are ready to meditate. Choose any one of the five presented in table 11.1.

Table 11.1   Selected meditations

Candle Flame Meditation

Gaze (do not stare) at the flame of a candle placed at least five feet away from you until your eyes close. Then, bring the picture of the flame, colors and movement all with you into meditation.

The Yes Meditation

Take in several deep, slow breaths to relax you. Visualize the word *yes* in large white print on a dark background. See it blink like a neon light, move to the left and disappear. Immediately following this first *yes* comes one, a little smaller. Repeat with each *yes* getting smaller and smaller for the count of ten *yesses* and then reverse the order until you return to the first *yes*. Now see a smaller *yes* appear. With each *yes*, see them getting smaller and smaller until you return to the original *yes*. Now, take in several deep, slow breaths to totally relax you.

Love Meditation

Close your eyes. Take a deep breath and relax. Visualize the word *love* in either a white or pink color. As you see this word, think of what it means to you and then picture someone you love with all your heart. Get into the feeling of love, and feel this beautiful emotion spread throughout your body and then center itself in the area of your heart. Imagine the energy of love emanating in the universe (yes, even to the difficult person you are caring for). Send the energy of love to that person. Notice and feel the positive change that takes place between yourself and that person. Get into this wonderful feeling, and bring it with you as you slowly open your eyes. Take a deep slow breath in and let it out slowly.

Breath Counting

Close your eyes, relax your body and breathe in and out several times deeply and slowly. Breathe in. Hearing in your mind, you breathe on the intake—one—on the out—two, in again—one, out again—two. Repeat this ten times and work it up to twenty. This meditation is fantastic for concentration and focusing.

Mini Vacation Meditation

Close your eyes. Breathe in through your nose; breathe out slowly through your mouth. Repeat. Now, feel yourself lift gently and start to travel. Picture in your mind a beautiful place that you would like to visit more than any other place: the seashore, the country or any place that makes you feel good. See it. Feel it. Breathe in the smells of nature. You can remain in your vacation place for as long as you wish. Now, take a deep breath in and let it out. Slowly, slowly, feel yourself back in the place where you started. Now open your eyes.

In addition to enhancing your self-awareness, you can take some other uncomplicated steps that can ease your caregiving stress. Since each of us is unique, honor and choose that which works best for you. While friends and colleagues may mean well and be full of advice and opinions, listen to your inner voice that tells you what's right for you. Remember that you may need to change as your situation changes, but do not give up your true self. Heraclitus said, "We never step into the same waters twice." His interpretation means that as much as we change as we step into the waters, so, too, do the waters change at each moment.

Thus, as the caregiving intensity moves up, down, and sideways, you go through contortions, too. But, there is a very positive, practical side to all of this. Change teaches you much about life and your competencies that you may never have learned before.

GAINING PERSPECTIVE: FINDING BALANCE

Not everything you need to do is complicated, expensive, exhausting or impossible. The first thing to remember is that you can only do the possible. As hard as the juggling act is, you need to find balance between your family, your career, the care recipient and yourself.

There are limits to what you can do. You cannot make everything right all the time. Your care recipient may have a medical condition that is not in your control. For example, while you cannot keep a cancer from spreading, you can address the care recipient's quality of life—by maintaining a nurturing environment, along with pain management, healthy nutrition and social stimulation. Accept the boundaries and work with them. Your cancer patient may enjoy some time outdoors to visit his or her garden by wheelchair. While this may not seem very significant to you, it may be a revitalizing interlude for the patient. Appreciate small victories.

Your own health concerns and care are not to be ignored at this time of heightened stress. Even though you're trying to do your best for the care recipient, you need to do everything to avoid becoming the second patient. Follow your prescribed regimens of diet, exercise and medications. Get needed sleep and rest. Stay connected to your social contacts. Do things that help you to unwind, and take time out for fun. And don't forget to take your emotional temperature.

YOUR EMOTIONAL HEALTH

Are emotions such as anxiety, guilt and anger spilling over? Do you feel depressed? Are these feelings interfering with your daily function—your relationships, your job, your sleep, your appetite, your health and your efficiency? If so, pay attention. While there is no "magic pill" to relieve your caregiving pressure, medical conditions such as significant depression and anxiety can develop and may require interventions including counseling, medications, natural or alternative therapies, lifestyle changes or combined approaches. When feeling overwrought, you may need to consult a professional.

Additional choices are available. Support groups—meetings of caregivers, peer or professionally led, provide opportunity to share experiences and practical tips, as well as vent feelings in a "safe" environment. For information about available support groups, a good first contact would be your local Office on Aging or disease-specific organizations, such as the Alzheimer's Association or Cancer Care. Not being a group person, you may seek individual counseling. Your physician or clergy members may be an additional resource.

DECOMPRESS

Take some time to think about how you can decompress. Use your self-awareness to guide you toward making it easier on yourself. Help is available. You can do the following: Hire a home health aide. Ask a sibling or relative to pitch in. Use additional services, such as adult day health care. Do a temporary respite placement. Or use a combination of any of the above. Feeling overburdened, you might not want to make even one more arrangement. You've had it.

If this is true for you, here's another option. Hire a professional geriatric care manager. A geriatric care manager can work with you and the family to provide a tailor-made menu of the best care for your elderly relative. Care managers can relieve your burden by doing the following:

- Assess the elder to determine his or her individualized needs, and develop a plan of care;
- Arrange for home help, that is, interview and select candidates, carefully matching the needs of the care recipient with the skills of the applicant;
- Make sure that the applicant is credible, reliable, appropriately screened and trained;
- Consistently supervise the home help via regular telephone contact and scheduled and nonanticipated visits;
- Order supplies such as durable medical equipment, diapers, nutritional supplements and clothing;
- Coordinate and serve as the essential link between all services;

- Make referrals to providers, such as adult day health care, physicians, dentists, laboratories, nutritionists, beauticians, therapists and counselors;
- Escort the care recipient to appointments;
- Identify facilities for placement, such as assisted living and nursing homes that best meet the needs and lifestyle of the care recipient;
- Ease the transition from home to facility;
- Supervise the after-placement care; and
- Work with the other professionals involved, such as physicians, lawyers, accountants and financial planners.

Working with you for as long as needed, the care manager is generally available as the intensity of needs changes. To locate a geriatric care manager in your relative's locale, telephone (520) 881-8008 or visit www.caremanager.org.

TAKE TIME OUT

Everybody needs some time away from the stresses and strains of caregiving. Maybe you should find out what your benefits are in terms of leave from your job—vacation, sabbatical, family leave—and see whether or not you can get some time off when things are boiling over. For example, Magda, an only child, was constantly receiving "panic calls" regarding her mom's health ups and downs and her being ricocheted back and forth from nursing home to hospital (or to rehabilitation center, to nursing home, to psychiatric ward) and back to nursing home. Even though Magda had placed her mother in a nursing home, it did not provide the relief she thought she would get from the day-to-day management.

Soon after placement, her mother's condition became unstable, and Magda chose to be there for her as much as she could. Not long after, Magda began to worry about whether she could continue to do this and also hold down her full-time job. Finding a creative solution, she discovered, with delight and surprise, that her employer would allow her to take "family leave" by the hour, so that she could parcel out her sick, vacation and family leave time, as needed. Knowing your options may give you more freedom.

Susan, who had also placed her mother in a nursing facility, did not experience the sudden changes in condition but did find herself wanting to visit often, at least three times a week, "to be there for my helpless mother." Intellectually, she knew that placement was appropriate, but emotionally she was uneasy, guilty and conflicted. While she has retired, her husband, Walt, maintains his consulting business almost "full speed" at age seventy. Empathic toward Susan, he is not thrilled with the situation. Their daughter, Abby, who lives two states away, has a fourteen-month-old baby girl, their first and only grandchild, whom they did not get to see much during her first few months because of their heavy eldercare responsibilities.

Realizing how much they have been missing, they have resolved to spend a long weekend each month with their daughter, granddaughter and son-in-law. This minivacation gives them a needed "lift," and they love watching this little person grow and flourish.

MAINTAIN YOUR RELATIONSHIPS

Your family is not only the original nuclear family but also includes your spouse or partner, children, grandchildren and other family members and friends that you have been close to. Says one husband,

> I've always loved my mother-in-law and understand my wife's devotion to her. But since she became a caregiver, she has little time for me. We almost never have sex. She's too tired. I'm constantly making dinners and caring for the kids because she's almost never around. I feel lost and neglected, and I worry about the impact on our marriage and the kids. How long will this go on?

To address these issues, the balance has to be reshifted. This caregiver must look at what is happening in her own household and her life and rethink her priorities. Maybe this is the time for her to demand that her siblings share the responsibilities, insisting that she "can no longer go it alone." Looking at the total picture is crucial.

SHARING RESPONSIBILITIES

Perhaps you are the designated primary caregiver. But that does not mean that you have to be the only one. A family is a conglomerate of people who need to work as a team. Just as successful corporations rely on teams, so, too, should the vulnerable elder be able to rely on an effective family team for care and protection. At this time, past conflicts are irrelevant. The problem at hand is what counts. The primary caregiver needs to accept help from family and friends, neighbors and professionals.

Make specific requests. Caregiving is a big job, and the primary care-giver should not be reluctant or unwilling to request help from other family members, friends and neighbors. Be specific as to what you need. Don't say, "You don't help me," which will be understood as accusatory, or even, "Can you help me out some time?" which is too general. Be clear and upfront about what you want. "Can you watch Mom Sundays from two to four o'clock, so that I can continue with my aerobics classes?" Or, as in the case of Dorothy who has Alzheimer's disease and wants to participate in a research study, her daughter-in-law, Carol, asked a neighbor who has a car and is currently not working if she could take Dorothy for her weekly visit for the next two months. If your care recipient is in a nursing home, encourage visits from others and use their visits as time for you to do other things—similarly, if there is a hospitalization.

LIGHTEN THE LOAD

Reset your expectations. You don't have to do everything the way you always did. Says one caregiver, "I used to want things to be perfect, but now I find that good enough is okay." Order routine prescriptions by mail and get the drugs for as many months as the insurance will allow. Likewise, with nutritional supplements, incontinence products and medical supplies, order them by phone or Internet and have them delivered. If the care recipient is homebound and requires frequent lab tests, such as when someone is on blood thinners, ask the physician to refer a laboratory that makes house calls. Some do. Happily, too, there are physicians who make home visits and even "mobile" dentists. And, if you request it, clergy members and congregants will do home visits.

ENJOY LEISURE PURSUITS

Leisure is in the eye of the beholder. While gardening may be fun for some, it's unwanted work for others. The point is, if you have been a horticultural enthusiast, find a way to continue. If you've always been an avid reader, again, find some time for this. You may choose to read to your care recipient if they can no longer read. And reading aloud to the care recipient is something your own teenager might enjoy. A further benefit is the bonding that will naturally occur.

Invest some energy and time in yourself. For some people, physical exercise such as jogging, swimming, walking or yoga is their joy. For others, massages, beauty treatments, long baths and naps replenish their energy and uplift their spirits. Music, dance and theatre may be your outlets of choice.

STAY COOL

You may expect the home health aide or your family care partners to arrive exactly on time every time, but this may not necessarily happen. Family situations arise. Transportation problems develop. Hopefully, they will call you in advance, but don't fly off the handle if they don't. Take a deep breath and evaluate the situation in terms of the larger picture. If this person is generally an asset and you want their continued help, be forgiving. You'll all be better off. Or, if your home help does not cook as well as you would like, try to give them specific instructions, simplify the menu or use more prepared foods. Again, evaluate the whole picture. What are they really there for—gourmet meals or the well-being and safety of the care recipient?

RESPITE CARE

At-home caregivers can integrate their "time out" with "time out" (respite) for the care recipient, as well. There are temporary stays available, usually scheduled in advance, in nursing homes, assisted living facilities, group homes or other such places. Typically, these stays are for several days to a month. Families may use respite for occasions such as an out-of-town wedding or graduation, when a caregiver has elective surgery or for a regularly scheduled vacation. Check out the availability in your area. Respite services can also be provided with home care, using a temporary, twenty-four-hour, live-in aide.

While some families can pay privately for respite, others may need to seek alternative sources of funding. In some states, this may be an included benefit for Medicaid recipients. State-funded disability programs may cover respite, and also some categorical disease associations, such as the Alzheimer's Association in some areas, may help. Hospice programs offer respite. And a respite benefit is included in some long-term care insurance policies.

In the case of Matthew, the attorney who became disabled by a stroke, Helen, his wife, chose to hire a home health aide to come to her home for a period of time to allow her the freedom to participate in the golf tournament to which she had committed. Or, as happened, Helen wanted to visit her childhood friend, Gretchen, who lived down South, for a few days during the winter. She was also able to arrange for a home health aide to live in and take care of Matthew while she was gone.

Adult day health programs (also called medical day care) are a good resource for providing respite for caregivers and socialization, nutritious meals, medication management, nursing supervision, rehabilitation, and transportation for the frail elder. Day health programs can be paid for privately or covered by long-term care insurance. For care recipients of limited means, entitlements such as Medicaid may pay for day health programs. A good source of information is your local Office on Aging. Another source to check out is Veterans' benefits for those who qualify. Attendance may range from two to five days per week. During times of high stress or illness of the caregiver, the number of days of attendance can be increased temporarily. Day programs are valuable for working caregivers.

SELF-CARE IS A RESPONSIBLE PRACTICE

Self-care as a healthy and valuable process is being widely discussed these days. Struggling with conflicts and deterrents to their own self-care, many caregivers are reluctant to offer themselves the same understanding and care they extend to others. Yet, in reality, self-care may be the most important thing that you do, not only for yourself but also for your care recipient. Certainly, self-care is a responsible practice—for all human beings involved in the care of others. You need renewal, nurturance and balance in order to be and stay an efficient and healthy caregiver.

· *12* ·

A Primer for
Demystifying the Maze

$\mathcal{C}$aregivers are suddenly faced with learning a foreign language: that of eldercare. We read the terms. What does it all mean? Medicare, Medicaid—are they the same or different? Home care, hospice—who is there to explain it all to me? A glossary of terms follows.

GLOSSARY

Activities of Daily Living (ADL)

Activities of Daily Living are those functions that are part of the daily routine. They include bathing, dressing, toileting, transferring, ambulating and eating. An individual's functional ability is measured by their capability to perform these functions. These are usually an important part of the criteria for qualifying for nursing home placement, Medicaid services in the community and long-term care insurance benefits.

Advance Directives

Individuals have a right to express their values and preferences regarding limiting or forgoing life-sustaining medical treatment. The Living Will and the Durable Power of Attorney for Health Care are the two common forms of advance directives. The Living Will states the individual's wishes regarding future health-care decisions. With the Durable Power of Attorney, the individual designates a surrogate (sometimes called a Health-Care Proxy) to make treatment decisions for them, if they lack decision-making capacity.

While advance directives are recognized in most states, there are variations, particularly as regards the use of artificial feeding and hydration.

Ageism

Ageism is a form of bigotry and prejudice directed at people simply because of their age. Certain stereotypes are prominent—loss of attractiveness, declines in physical and mental abilities, and loss of sexual interest and abilities. Unfortunately, ageism is deeply ingrained in our culture and is partially a result of intergenerational competition for jobs and resources. Because of the stigma, older people tend to try to conceal their age and remain as much a part of the mainstream as possible. Ironically, older people themselves tend to have negative attitudes toward themselves and other elders.

Assisted Living

Assisted living is housing enmeshed with services. Unlike nursing homes, where there is a panoply of services for every resident, assisted living residents can choose and pay for only the services they need. Generally, the elder resides in a suite or small apartment, shared or not shared, and receives a basic package of services, including housekeeping, meals, nursing supervision, activities and local transportation. Additional services that can be purchased include medication administration, assistance with personal care and nursing services. Residents can bring their furniture and automobile.

Some assisted living facilities have specialized dementia units, which vary regarding environmental features, including services, staff training and cost. Funding for assisted living is generally by self-payment, although some states provide Medicaid assistance and many long-term care insurance policies cover this level of care.

Burn-out

Burn-out is a negative outcome for health-care workers and family caregivers who often work under very stressful conditions. It affects attitudes and performance and results in diminished quality of care.

Continuing Care Retirement Communities (CCRC)

CCRCs are providers of housing and multiple levels of "life care" for their residents. Usually in a campus setting, services include independent living, assisted living, health monitoring, home care, nursing home care and even specialized dementia services. Some also have their own medical staff and clinics. While some CCRCs are quite upscale, others are more moderate. An entry fee is generally required as well as regular monthly payments. Residents are able to avail themselves of a spectrum of care in a familiar and comfortable community, and their monthly fees do not necessarily rise with increasing care needs, thus shielding against depletion of assets by catastrophic long-term care costs. This is made possible by sometimes substantial entry fees that are used to capitalize and subsidize the operations. Many CCRCs now offer a variety of financing options, and entry fees, monthly fees and additional costs vary with different arrangements.

Copayments

An insurance term, copayments refer to cost sharing that occurs between the insured and the insurer. For Medicare beneficiaries enrolled in part B (medical insurance), Medicare pays 80 percent of allowable charges, and the insured pays the 20 percent balance. Under part A (hospital insurance), there is an annual deductible and then a copayment for days 61–90 and a higher copayment from day 91 to a lifetime maximum. For nursing home care under part A, the first twenty days in a benefit period are covered fully, with a copay required beginning at day 21, to a maximum of one hundred days, if the patient meets Medicare diagnosis and treatment need criteria. Medigap policies generally cover deductibles and copayments, but these benefits are determined by the type of medigap plan purchased. Some policies also will pay excess physician fees under part B.

Custodial Care

Medicare specifically does not pay for "custodial services"—supervision and help with the Activities of Daily Living, including bathing, dressing, eating, toileting, walking and other daily tasks. These service needs are generally on-going, and the frail elders needing this help may actually require only limited skilled nursing care. These services can be provided in the home by home health aides, in nursing homes by certified nursing assistants or in assisted living facilities by personal care staff. Custodial care may be covered by Medicaid, by Veterans' benefits and long-term care insurance, or by the elder or family.

Deductibles

In addition to copayments in insurance, deductibles are another form of cost sharing. In Medicare, they refer to an amount that must be paid by the beneficiary before Medicare will pick up the tab. With long-term care insurance, a deductible can be described as an elimination period during which you are the payer. This period begins after you have met the qualifying medical criteria.

Delirium

Delirium is an acute mental change that usually manifests with sudden and severe confusion, fluctuating awareness and attention, and even hallucinations. Usually associated with an underlying illness such as infection, dehydration, a medication reaction or surgery, it affects community-based and hospitalized elders, especially those with dementia. Delirium can be life threatening and requires prompt medical intervention.

Dementia

Dementia is a progressive decline in memory and other intellectual functions, severe enough to interfere with daily function. There are associated declines in Activities of Daily Living and behavior and changes in personality and mood. The declines represent changes from a prior level of function. While dementia may be caused by a number of conditions, Alzheimer's disease is the most common in the elderly. While all individuals with Alzheimer's disease have a dementia, all individuals with dementia do not necessarily have Alzheimer's disease.

Depression

Depression is a psychiatric illness whose symptoms may include a low mood with lack of interest, lack of energy, loss of appetite, pain, changes in sleep pattern, bodily preoccupations, pain, and feelings of hopelessness and worthlessness. Suicide is a potentially lethal outcome. Depression may masquerade as or mimic dementia or occur concurrently.

Do Not Resuscitate (DNR)

Do not resuscitate is a physician's order for no resuscitative attempts in the event of a cardiac or respiratory arrest, in cases where resuscitation would be medically inappropriate. In health-care facilities, the order is developed in compliance with the patient's or surrogate's wishes and is documented in the medical record. The patient, surrogate or physician may rescind it at any time. In states where it is permissible, individuals residing at home can make the DNR decision as well, complete and sign a form that the doctor also signs and post it conspicuously for all emergency medical services personnel.

Durable Medical Equipment (DME)

Special equipment such as wheelchairs, hospital beds and oxygen pumps, which enable an elder to be cared for at home are called DME. These items and medical supplies, including splints and dressings, are covered by Medicare, if they are prescribed by a physician and provided through a certified medical equipment provider. If equipment or supplies are provided in conjunction with skilled home care covered under part A, then Medicare pays 100 percent; if not, part B pays 80 percent of the approved charges.

Entitlements

Entitlements are benefits that are available to all individuals who meet their eligibility criteria. Medicare, Medicaid and Veterans' benefits are examples.

Home Health Care

Whether due to illness, frailty or a combination, many elders need care and assistance beyond the informal care that is provided by their families, friends and neighbors. Some service needs may be time limited, others long term. While these services are available in nursing homes and other facilities, the majority of elders prefer to receive needed assistance in the comfort of their own homes. Home health care includes skilled nursing services and custodial care. Payment sources include self-payment, Medicare and other health insurance, long-term care insurance, Veterans' benefits and Medicaid, with the entitlement and insurance programs having their own criteria. So strong is their preference for home care that elders vote with their pocketbooks, assuming these costs privately.

Hospice

Normally offered to individuals who are terminally ill with a life expectancy of less than six months, hospice provides comprehensive palliative care and support services, including bereavement counseling for family members. Hospice patients do not receive aggressive life-sustaining treatments such as antibiotics, cardiopulmonary resuscitation (CPR), and artificial nutrition and hydration. Pain management, however, is a high priority. Hospice patients are cared for most often in the home, but some are in assisted living facilities and nursing homes. Hospice is a covered benefit under Medicare part A. While the hospice patient elects to give up the right for Medicare to pay for other services to treat the terminal illness, Medicare pays the hospice and related physician fees and will continue to pay for any services not related to the terminal illness. Private insurance and Veterans' benefits also pay for hospice.

Informed Consent

Informed consent for medical treatment is given only after the patient or his or her surrogate have been given a detailed explanation of the nature, risks, benefits and alternatives to a medical treatment or research study.

Living Will

A Living Will is a document that expresses an individual's wishes for future medical care and may include information about wishes for or against life-sustaining or invasive measures and artificial feeding and nutrition. This may be a separate document or be incorporated into a Durable Power of Attorney for Health Care. Format and rules differ among the states, and individuals should seek accurate information when planning to relocate to another state. Additionally, this document should be reviewed regularly to assure that it is consistent with the individual's current wishes.

Long-Term Care

Long-term care refers to ongoing health- and personal-care services needed to help an individual function as well as possible. Many people automatically associate long-term care with "nursing home." While long-term care includes nursing home care, it also includes assisted living and a spectrum of home and community-based care. Services for the elderly differ in form and duration, and the needs of an individual may change over time. While sick and disabled individuals of any age may require long-term care services, the biggest users are frail elders.

Long-Term Care Insurance

Long-term care insurance is different from other health insurance and from life insurance. A long-term care policy provides protection in case you need long-term care. In general, these private policies are reimbursement plans, paying a defined amount for care received, for a defined amount of time—for example, one hundred dollars per day for up to five years. Long-term care policies differ in benefits they offer and premiums. Generally, the younger you are when you buy a policy, the lower your premiums. Long-term care insurance is not for everyone and should be incorporated into an overall financial planning process.

Look Back Period

At the time of application for Medicaid benefits, the Medicaid agency will require submission of five years of financial records to determine whether any assets have been sold or given away during this period, which is called the "look back period." If any unallowable transfers are identified during this time frame, eligibility for Medicaid will be delayed. The look back period was extended by federal legislation in 2006. Given the concerns regarding cost containment on both the federal and state levels and the potential for other changes, it is important to get accurate, current information before starting the Medicaid application process.

Medicaid

Medicaid, established in 1965, is jointly financed by the federal government and the states. Targeted to the poor, Medicaid is a safety-net program that helps support the health and long-term care services infrastructure for all. Under Medicaid, access is ensured for health and nursing home care for the elderly, disabled individuals and children in households having both low income and assets.

Medicaid eligibility requires a "means test," that is, applicants must meet income and asset requirements, in addition to medical need. There are wide disparities among state programs. While three-quarters of its eldercare funds are channeled to institutional care, Medicaid programs may include some funding for home and community-based services for the elderly, such as home care and adult day health-care programs, as alternatives to nursing home care. Overall, Medicaid is the source of payments for 47 percent of nursing home expenditures. For the elderly, Medicaid benefits are provided in addition to Medicare health insurance.

For eligibility information, contact the local Office on Aging or the Department of Human Services, where the elder resides. General information about Medicaid is available online, at no cost, from the American Association of Retired Persons (AARP) at www.aarp.org/research/health/medicaid.

Medicare

Medicare is federally sponsored health insurance for Americans who are sixty-five and older and qualify for Social Security retirement benefits, and those under sixty-five who are disabled or have end-stage kidney disease. The hospital benefit (part A) is provided for all who qualify at no cost. The medical services benefit (part B) is optional and available for a monthly premium. Part D, prescription drug coverage, new in 2006, is also optional and requires a separate enrollment and a monthly premium. While Medicare provides very valuable coverage, there are gaps. Some of these gaps, such as deductibles and copayments, can be met through medigap insurance. One of the largest gaps in the program is long-term nursing home care. Only very short-term coverage is provided under Medicare, following a three-day hospital stay at least, and meeting other specified requirements. Medigap does not cover any more long-term care than Medicare. Information about Medicare is available from www.medicare.gov.

Medigap Insurance

Medicare enrollees can purchase supplemental insurance policies (medigap) from a private insurance company to cover the gaps in Medicare, such as the deductibles and copayments. While policies differ, a separate premium is required for this coverage, and it is guaranteed renewable as long as the premium is paid. Medigap policies are standardized and must follow federal and state laws. To buy a medigap policy, an individual must have Medicare part A and part B in the original Medicare plan.

Nursing Homes

Nursing homes provide medical care, nursing care, supervision and personal care for people who generally have several chronic conditions and impairments in their Activities of Daily Living and are unable to care for themselves or be maintained at home. About 10 percent of the nursing home population is under age sixty-five. Of those over sixty-five, the majority are over eighty. The majority of nursing home residents have cognitive problems.

Respite

Respite essentially means time out for the caregiver. This may be done with temporary placement of the care recipient in a nursing home or Assisted Living Facility or hiring temporary round-the-clock help to enable the caregiver to get a break from caregiving responsibilities, whether for a vacation, a family celebration, a family emergency, elective surgery or just some time off. Adult day health centers, whereby the elder attends a day program that provides her or him with socialization, meals, activities, medication management and transportation, can provide a break for the caregiver, especially the working caregiver.

Reverse Mortgage

A reverse mortgage is a loan, available to persons over sixty-two years old, enabling them to borrow money against the equity that they have in their home. This loan is special because it does not encumber them with monthly payments. Rather, repayment of the loan and cumulative interest is postponed until the borrower moves, sells the house or dies. While reverse mortgages are not for everyone, they are a means of supplementing retirement income.

Spend Down

While financial eligibility criteria are different for each state's Medicaid program, all programs have income and asset limits. Meeting the asset limit is the most difficult part of the process. If you have assets above the limit, you can either transfer or restructure your assets, if you do this well in advance of needing Medicaid. Or, you must spend down your savings and assets to the limit permitted in your state. There are certain assets that are exempt from these limits, such as household goods, one automobile, a burial plot and a small burial fund, and a very limited amount of funds, but these vary among states. In most states, the primary residence is exempt if a spouse or dependent still lives in it; however, some states will place a lien on the property. Realize that Medicaid continually faces the threat of changes, as policy makers look to cut tight budgets. It would, therefore, be wise to consult with experts in your relative's area to learn about the most updated rules.

Index

About the Authors

Miriam K. Aronson, Ed.D., a founder of the national Alzheimer's Association, was also the founding chair of its Education and Public Awareness Committee. A social gerontologist, Dr. Aronson has authored and coauthored many peer-reviewed publications in professional journals, has been a contributor to several books, and has edited three books, including *Reshaping Dementia Care: Practice and Policy in Long-Term Care*, winner of the National Nursing Association Book of the Year Award, and has given more than two hundred seminars and presentations nationally and internationally. She has worked extensively with individuals, families, and eldercare facilities to guide them through the caregiving process. Dr. Aronson is a member of the clinical faculty of the Albert Einstein College of Medicine and a fellow of the Gerontological Society of America and the American Orthopsychiatric Association.

Marcella Bakur Weiner, Ph.D, is a fellow of the American Psychological Association and an active member of its media division. Dr. Weiner has made numerous appearances on major TV networks and has been widely interviewed for primetime radio shows and popular magazines and newspapers including the *New York Times*, *New York Post*, the *Daily News*, and others. She also cohosted her own radio talk show. She is the author or coauthor of twenty books and seventy-five articles; her first book, *Working with the Aged* (1979), was considered a pioneer in its field. A fellow of the Gerontological Society of America and a practicing psychotherapist, she continues to be a leader in focusing on older adults and their families in her practice. Dr. Weiner is an adjunct professor at Marymount Manhattan College, teaching courses on working with older adults and their families.